Edgar Allan Poe
Fifty-four Poems

The Best of E. A. Poe Poetry

edit by

ISBN:9781802210248

Content

Preface 5
Poems Of Later Life 6
- The Raven 7
- The Bells 11
- Ulalume 14
- To Helen 17
- Annabel Lee 19
- A Valentine 21
- An Enigma 22
- For Annie 23
- To F-- 25
- To Frances S. Osgood 26
- Eldorado 27
- Eulalie 28
- A Dream Within A Dream 30
- To Marie Louise (Shew) I 31
- To Marie Louise (Shew) II 32
- The City In The Sea 33
- The Sleeper 35
- Bridal Ballad 37

Poems Of Manhood.. 38
- The Coliseum 39
- Lenore 41
- To One In Paradise... 43
- The Haunted Palace.. 44
- The Conqueror Worm 46
- Silence 47
- Dream-Land 48
- Hymn 50
- To Zante 51
- Scenes From "Politian" 52

Poems Of Youth 69
- Sonnet—To Science 70
- Letter To Mr. B— 71
- Al Aaraaf 80
- Tamerlane 98
- To Helen 105
- The Valley Of Unrest 106
- Israfel* 107
- To ——II 109
- To ——III 110
- To The River—— 111

- Song 112
- Spirits Of The Dead 113
- A Dream 114
- Romance 115
- Fairy-Land 116
- The Lake — To—— 118
- Evening Star 119
- "The Happiest Day" 120
- Imitation 121
- Hymn To Aristogeiton And Harmodius 122
- Dreams 123
- "In Youth I Have Known One" 124

Doubtful Poems 127
- The Forest Reverie 128
- Alone 129
- To Isadore 130
- The Village Street 132

Preface

Edgar Allan Poe is widely regarded as a central figure of Romanticism in the United States, and of American literature. Poe was one of the country's earliest practitioners of the short story and considered to be the inventor of the detective fiction genre, as well as a significant contributor to the emerging genre of science fiction.
While Poe is most often remembered for his short fiction, his first love as a writer was poetry, which he began writing during his adolescence.
The poem is still one of Poe's better efforts from his early years of writing poetry.
"Tamerlane" and "Al Aaraaf" exemplify Poe's evolution from the portrayal of Byronic heroes to the depiction of journeys within his own imagination and subconscious.
In other poems—"To Helen," "Lenore," and "The Raven" in particular—Poe investigates the loss of ideal beauty and the difficulty in regaining it.
These pieces are usually narrated by a young man who laments the untimely death of his beloved.
"To Helen" is a three-stanza lyric that has been called one of the most beautiful love poems in the English language. The subject of the work is a woman who becomes, in the eyes of the narrator, a personification of the classical beauty of ancient Greece and Rome. "Lenore" presents ways in which the dead are best remembered, either by mourning or celebrating life beyond earthly boundaries. In "The Raven," Poe successfully unites his philosophical and aesthetic ideals. In this psychological piece, a young scholar is emotionally tormented by a raven's ominous repetition of "Nevermore" in answer to his question about the probability of an afterlife with his deceased lover.

Poems Of Later Life

The Raven

Once upon a midnight dreary, while I pondered, weak and weary, Over many a quaint and curious volume of forgotten lore,
While I nodded, nearly napping, suddenly there came a tapping, As of some one gently rapping, rapping at my chamber door. "'Tis some visiter," I muttered, "tapping at my chamber door—
Only this, and nothing more."

Ah, distinctly I remember it was in the bleak December,
And each separate dying ember wrought its ghost upon the floor. Eagerly I wished the morrow;—vainly I had sought to borrow From my books surcease of sorrow—sorrow for the lost Lenore— For the rare and radiant maiden whom the angels name Lenore—
Nameless here for evermore.

And the silken sad uncertain rustling of each purple curtain
Thrilled me—filled me with fantastic terrors never felt before;
So that now, to still the beating of my heart, I stood repeating
"'Tis some visiter entreating entrance at my chamber door—
Some late visiter entreating entrance at my chamber door;—
This it is, and nothing more."

Presently my soul grew stronger; hesitating then no longer,
"Sir," said I, "or Madam, truly your forgiveness I implore;
But the fact is I was napping, and so gently you came rapping,
And so faintly you came tapping, tapping at my chamber door,
That I scarce was sure I heard you "—here I opened wide the door;—— Darkness there and nothing more.

Deep into that darkness peering, long I stood there wondering, fearing, Doubting, dreaming dreams no mortal ever dared to dream before;

But the silence was unbroken, and the darkness gave no token,
And the only word there spoken was the whispered word,
"Lenore!"
This I whispered, and an echo murmured back the word,
"Lenore!"— Merely this, and nothing more.

Back into the chamber turning, all my soul within me burning,
Soon I heard again a tapping somewhat louder than before.

"Surely," said I, "surely that is something at my window lattice;
Let me see, then, what thereat is, and this mystery explore—
Let my heart be still a moment and this mystery explore;—
'Tis the wind and nothing more!"

Open here I flung the shutter, when, with many a flirt and flutter, In there stepped a stately raven of the saintly days of yore;
Not the least obeisance made he; not an instant stopped or stayed he; But, with mien of lord or lady, perched above my chamber door— Perched upon a bust of Pallas just above my chamber door—
Perched, and sat, and nothing more.

Then this ebony bird beguiling my sad fancy into smiling,
By the grave and stern decorum of the countenance it wore,
"Though thy crest be shorn and shaven, thou," I said, "art sure no craven, Ghastly grim and ancient raven wandering from the Nightly shore—
Tell me what thy lordly name is on the Night's Plutonian shore!" Quoth the raven "Nevermore."

Much I marvelled this ungainly fowl to hear discourse so plainly, Though its answer little meaning—little relevancy bore;
For we cannot help agreeing that no living human being Ever yet was blessed with seeing bird above his chamber door— Bird or beast upon the sculptured bust above his chamber door,
With such name as "Nevermore."

But the raven, sitting lonely on the placid bust, spoke only
That one word, as if his soul in that one word he did outpour.
Nothing farther then he uttered—not a feather then he fluttered—
Till I scarcely more than muttered "Other friends have flown before— On the morrow he will leave me, as my hopes have flown before."
Then the bird said "Nevermore."

Startled at the stillness broken by reply so aptly spoken,
"Doubtless," said I, "what it utters is its only stock and store
Caught from some unhappy master whom unmerciful Disaster
Followed fast and followed faster till his songs one burden bore— Till the dirges of his Hope that melancholy burden bore
Of "Never—nevermore."

But the raven still beguiling all my sad soul into smiling,
Straight I wheeled a cushioned seat in front of bird, and bust and door; Then, upon the velvet sinking, I betook myself to linking

Fancy unto fancy, thinking what this ominous bird of yore—
What this grim, ungainly, ghastly, gaunt and ominous bird of yore
Meant in croaking "Nevermore."

This I sat engaged in guessing, but no syllable expressing
To the fowl whose fiery eyes now burned into my bosom's core; This and more I sat divining, with my head at ease reclining
On the cushion's velvet lining that the lamplght gloated o'er,
But whose velvet violet lining with the lamplight gloating o'er,
She shall press, ah, nevermore!

Then, methought, the air grew denser, perfumed from an unseen censer Swung by Angels whose faint foot-falls tinkled on the tufted floor. "Wretch," I cried, "thy God hath lent thee— by these angels he hath sent thee
Respite—respite and nepenthe from thy memories of Lenore;
Quaff, oh quaff this kind nepenthe and forget this lost Lenore!"
Quoth the raven, "Nevermore."

"Prophet!" said I, "thing of evil!—prophet still, if bird or devil!—
Whether Tempter sent, or whether tempest tossed thee here ashore, Desolate ye t all undaunted, on this desert land enchanted—
On this home by Horror haunted—tell me truly, I implore—
Is there—is there balm in Gilead?—tell me—tell me, I implore!"
Quoth the raven, "Nevermore."

"Prophet!" said I, "thing of evil—prophet still, if bird or devil!
By that Heaven that bends above us—by that God we both adore— Tell this soul with sorrow laden if, within the distant Aidenn,
It shall clasp a sainted maiden whom the angels name Lenore— Clasp a rare and radiant maiden whom the angels name Lenore." Quoth the raven, "Nevermore."

"Be that word our sign of parting, bird or fiend!" I shrieked, upstarting— "Get thee back into the tempest and the Night's Plutonian shore!
Leave no black plume as a token of that lie thy soul hath spoken! Leave my loneliness unbroken!—quit the bust above my door!
Take thy beak from out my heart, and take thy form from off my door!" Quoth the raven, "Nevermore."

And the raven, never flitting, still is sitting, still is sitting On the pallid bust of Pallas just above my chamber door;
And his eyes have all the seeming of a demon's that is dreaming, And the lamp-light o'er him streaming throws his shadow on the floor; And my soul from out that shadow that lies floating on the floor
Shall be lifted—nevermore!

The Bells

I.
HEAR the sledges with the bells— Silver bells!
What a world of merriment their melody foretells!
How they tinkle, tinkle, tinkle, In the icy air of night!
While the stars that oversprinkle All the heavens, seem to twinkle With a crystalline delight;
Keeping time, time, time, In a sort of Runic rhyme,
To the tintinnabulation that so musically wells From the bells, bells, bells, bells,
Bells, bells, bells—
From the jingling and the tinkling of the bells.
II.
Hear the mellow wedding-bells Golden bells!
What a world of happiness their harmony foretells!
Through the balmy air of night How they ring out their delight!—
From the molten-golden notes, And all in tune,
What a liquid ditty floats
To the turtle-dove that listens, while she gloats On the moon!
Oh, from out the sounding cells, What a gush of euphony voluminously wells!
How it swells! How it dwells
On the Future!—how it tells Of the rapture that impels
To the swinging and the ringing Of the bells, bells, bells—
Of the bells, bells, bells, bells,
Bells, bells, bells—
To the rhyming and the chiming of the bells!
III.
Hear the loud alarum bells— Brazen bells!
What tale of terror, now, their turbulency tells!
In the startled ear of night
How they scream out their affright!
Too much horrified to speak, They can only shriek, shriek,
Out of tune,
In a clamorous appealing to the mercy of the fire,

In a mad expostulation with the deaf and frantic fire, Leaping higher, higher, higher,
With a desperate desire, And a resolute endeavor Now—now to sit, or never,
By the side of the pale-faced moon.
Oh, the bells, bells, bells! What a tale their terror tells
Of Despair!
How they clang, and clash, and roar! What a horror they outpour
On the bosom of the palpitating air!
Yet the ear, it fully knows, By the twanging
And the clanging,
How the danger ebbs and flows; Yet, the ear distinctly tells,
In the jangling
And the wrangling,
How the danger sinks and swells,
By the sinking or the swelling in the anger of the bells— Of the bells—
Of the bells, bells, bells, bells,
Bells, bells, bells—
In the clamour and the clangour of the bells!
IV.
Hear the tolling of the bells— Iron bells!
What a world of solemn thought their monody compels!
In the silence of the night, How we shiver with affright
At the melancholy meaning of their tone!
For every sound that floats From the rust within their throats
Is a groan.
And the people—ah, the people— They that dwell up in the steeple,
All alone,
And who, tolling, tolling, tolling, In that muffled monotone,
Feel a glory in so rolling
On the human heart a stone— They are neither man nor woman— They are neither brute nor human—
They are Ghouls:—
And their king it is who tolls:— And he rolls, rolls, rolls, rolls,
Rolls
A pæan from the bells!
And his merry bosom swells With the pæan of the bells!
And he dances, and he yells; Keeping time, time, time,

In a sort of Runic rhyme,
To the pæan of the bells— Of the bells:—
Keeping time, time, time, In a sort of Runic rhyme,
To the throbbing of the bells— Of the bells, bells, bells—
To the sobbing of the bells:— Keeping time, time, time,
As he knells, knells, knells, In a happy Runic rhyme,
To the rolling of the bells— Of the bells, bells, bells:—
To the tolling of the bells— Of the bells, bells, bells, bells,
Bells, bells, bells—
To the moaning and the groaning of the bells.

 Ulalume

The skies they were ashen and sober;
The leaves they were crisped and sere— The leaves they were withering and sere;
It was night in the lonesome October Of my most immemorial year:
It was hard by the dim lake of Auber, In the misty mid region of Weir:—
It was down by the dank tarn of Auber,
In the ghoul-haunted woodland of Weir.
Here once, through an alley Titanic,
Of cypress, I roamed with my Soul— Of cypress, with Psyche, my Soul.
There were days when my heart was volcanic As the scoriac rivers that roll—
As the lavas that restlessly roll
Their sulphurous currents down Yaanek, In the ultimate climes of the Pole—
That groan as they roll down Mount Yaanek In the realms of the Boreal Pole.
Our talk had been serious and sober,
But our thoughts they were palsied and sere— Our memories were treacherous and sere;
For we knew not the month was October, And we marked not the night of the year— (Ah, night of all nights in the year!)
We noted not the dim lake of Auber,
(Though once we had journeyed down here) We remembered not the dank tarn of Auber,
Nor the ghoul-haunted woodland of Weir.

And now, as the night was senescent, And star-dials pointed to morn— As the star-dials hinted of morn—
At the end of our path a liquescent And nebulous lustre was born,
 Out of which a miraculous crescent Arose with a duplicate horn—
Astarte's bediamonded crescent, Distinct with its duplicate horn.

And I said—"She is warmer than Dian: She rolls through an ether of sighs— She revels in a region of sighs.
She has seen that the tears are not dry on These cheeks, where the worm never dies,
And has come past the stars of the Lion, To point us the path to the skies—
To the Lethean peace of the skies— Come up, in despite of the Lion,
To shine on us with her bright eyes— Come up, through the lair of the Lion,
With love in her luminous eyes."
But Psyche, uplifting her finger, Said—"Sadly this star I mistrust— Her pallor I strangely mistrust—
Ah, hasten!—ah, let us not linger!
Ah, fly!—let us fly!—for we must." In terror she spoke; letting sink her
Wings till they trailed in the dust— In agony sobbed, letting sink her
Plumes till they trailed in the dust— Till they sorrowfully trailed in the dust.
I replied—"This is nothing but dreaming.
Let us on, by this tremulous light! Let us bathe in this crystalline light!
Its Sybillic splendor is beaming
With Hope and in Beauty to-night—
See!—it flickers up the sky through the night!
Ah, we safely may trust to its gleaming, And be sure it will lead us aright—
We safely may trust to a gleaming That cannot but guide us aright,
Since it flickers up to Heaven through the night."
Thus I pacified Psyche and kissed her, And tempted her out of her gloom—
 And conquered her scruples and gloom; And we passed to the end of the vista—
But were stopped by the door of a tomb— By the door of a legended tomb:—
And I said—"What is written, sweet sister, On the door of this legended tomb?" She replied—"Ulalume—Ulalume—
'T is the vault of thy lost Ulalume!"
Then my heart it grew ashen and sober

As the leaves that were crisped and sere— As the leaves that were withering and sere—
And I cried—"It was surely October On this very night of last year,
That I journeyed—I journeyed down here!— That I brought a dread burden down here— On this night, of all nights in the year,
Ah, what demon has tempted me here? Well I know, now, this dim lake of Auber—
This misty mid region of Weir:—
Well I know, now, this dank tarn of Auber— This ghoul-haunted woodland of Weir."

To Helen

I saw thee once—once only—years ago: I must not say how many—but not many. It was a July midnight; and from out
A full-orbed moon, that, like thine own soul, soaring, Sought a precipitate pathway up through heaven, There fell a silvery-silken veil of light,
With quietude, and sultriness, and slumber, Upon the upturned faces of a thousand Roses that grew in an enchanted garden,
Where no wind dared to stir, unless on tiptoe— Fell on the upturn'd faces of these roses
That gave out, in return for the love-light, Their odorous souls in an ecstatic death— Fell on the upturn'd faces of these roses
That smiled and died in this parterre, enchanted By thee, and by the poetry of thy presence.
Clad all in white, upon a violet bank
I saw thee half reclining; while the moon Fell on the upturn'd faces of the roses,
And on thine own, upturn'd—alas, in sorrow!
Was it not Fate, that, on this July midnight- Was it not Fate, (whose name is also Sorrow,) That bade me pause before that garden-gate,
To breathe the incense of those slumbering roses? No footstep stirred: the hated world an slept, Save only thee and me. (Oh, Heaven!—oh, God!
How my heart beats in coupling those two words!) Save only thee and me. I paused—I looked-
And in an instant all things disappeared.
(Ah, bear in mind this garden was enchanted!)
The pearly lustre of the moon went out:
The mossy banks and the meandering paths, The happy flowers and the repining trees, Were seen no more: the very roses' odors
 Died in the arms of the adoring airs.
All—all expired save thee—save less than thou: Save only the divine light in thine eyes-
Save but the soul in thine uplifted eyes.

I saw but them—they were the world to me! I saw but them—saw only them for hours, Saw only them until the moon went down.
What wild heart-histories seemed to he enwritten
Upon those crystalline, celestial spheres! How dark a woe, yet how sublime a hope! How silently serene a sea of pride!
How daring an ambition; yet how deep- How fathomless a capacity for love!
But now, at length, dear Dian sank from sight, Into a western couch of thunder-cloud;
And thou, a ghost, amid the entombing trees Didst glide away. Only thine eyes remained; They would not go—they never yet have gone; Lighting my lonely pathway home that night,
They have not left me (as my hopes have) since;
They follow me—they lead me through the years. They are my ministers—yet I their slave.
Their office is to illumine and enkindle— My duty, to be saved by their bright light, And purified in their electric fire,
And sanctified in their elysian fire.
They fill my soul with Beauty (which is Hope), And are far up in Heaven—the stars I kneel to In the sad, silent watches of my night;
While even in the meridian glare of day I see them still—two sweetly scintillant Venuses, unextinguished by the sun!

Annabel Lee

It was many and many a year ago, In a kingdom by the sea,
That a maiden lived whom you may know By the name of
ANNABEL LEE;—
And this maiden she lived with no other thought Than to love
and be loved by me.
I was a child and She was a child, In this kingdom by the sea,
But we loved with a love that was more than love— I and my
ANNABEL LEE—
With a love that the wingèd seraphs of Heaven Coveted her
and me.
And this was the reason that, long ago, In this kingdom by the
sea,
A wind blew out of a cloud by night Chilling my ANNABEL
LEE;
So that her high-born kinsmen came And bore her away from
me,
To shut her up, in a sepulchre In this kingdom by the sea.
The angels, not half so happy in Heaven, Went envying her
and me;
Yes! that was the reason (as all men know, In this kingdom by
the sea)
That the wind came out of the cloud, chilling And killing my
ANNABEL LEE.
But our love it was stronger by far than the love Of those who
were older than we—
Of many far wiser than we—
And neither the angels in Heaven above Nor the demons
down under the sea Can ever dissever my soul from the soul
Of the beautiful ANNABEL LEE:—
 For the moon never beams without bringing me dreams Of
the beautiful ANNABEL LEE;
And the stars never rise but I see the bright eyes Of the
beautiful ANNABEL LEE;
And so, all the night-tide, I lie down by the side Of my
darling, my darling, my life and my bride

In her sepulchre there by the sea— In her tomb by the side of the sea.

A Valentine

For her this rhyme is penned, whose luminous eyes, Brightly expressive as the twins of Loeda,
Shall find her own sweet name, that, nestling lies Upon the page, enwrapped from every reader.
Search narrowly the lines!—they hold a treasure Divine—a talisman—an amulet
That must be worn at heart. Search well the measure— The words—the syllables! Do not forget
The trivialest point, or you may lose your labor!
And yet there is in this no Gordian knot

Which one might not undo without a sabre, If one could merely comprehend the plot.
Enwritten upon the leaf where now are peering Eyes scintillating soul, there lie perdus
Three eloquent words oft uttered in the hearing
Of poets, by poets—as the name is a poet's, too.
Its letters, although naturally lying
Like the knight Pinto—Mendez Ferdinando— Still form a synonym for Truth—Cease trying!
You will not read the riddle, though you do the best you can do.
1846.
[To discover the names in this and the following poem read the first letter of the first line in connection with the second letter of the second line, the third letter of the third line, the fourth of the fourth and so on to the end.]

# An Enigma

"Seldom we find," says Solomon Don Dunce, "Half an idea in the profoundest sonnet.
Through all the flimsy things we see at once As easily as through a Naples bonnet— Trash of all trash!—how can a lady don it?
Yet heavier far than your Petrarchan stuff- Owl-downy nonsense that the faintest puff
Twirls into trunk-paper the while you con it." And, veritably, Sol is right enough.
The general tuckermanities are arrant Bubbles—ephemeral and so transparent—
But this is, now,—you may depend upon it— Stable, opaque, immortal—all by dint
Of the dear names that lie concealed within 't.
1847. TO MY MOTHER

Because I feel that, in the Heavens above, The angels, whispering to one another,
Can find, among their burning terms of love, None so devotional as that of "Mother,"
Therefore by that dear name I long have called you— You who are more than mother unto me,
And fill my heart of hearts, where Death installed you In setting my Virginia's spirit free.
My mother—my own mother, who died early, Was but the mother of myself; but you
Are mother to the one I loved so dearly,
And thus are dearer than the mother I knew By that infinity with which my wife
Was dearer to my soul than its soul-life.
1849.
[The above was addressed to the poet's mother-in-law, Mrs. Clemm—Ed.]

For Annie

Thank Heaven! the crisis— The danger is past,
And the lingering illness Is over at last—
And the fever called "Living" Is conquered at last.
Sadly, I know
I am shorn of my strength, And no muscle I move
As I lie at full length— But no matter!—I feel
I am better at length.
And I rest so composedly, Now, in my bed,
That any beholder
Might fancy me dead— Might start at beholding me,
Thinking me dead.
The moaning and groaning, The sighing and sobbing,
Are quieted now,
With that horrible throbbing At heart:—ah, that horrible,
Horrible throbbing!
The sickness—the nausea— The pitiless pain—
Have ceased, with the fever That maddened my brain—
With the fever called "Living" That burned in my brain.
And oh! of all tortures
That torture the worst
 Has abated—the terrible Torture of thirst
For the naphthaline river Of Passion accurst:—
I have drank of a water
That quenches all thirst:—
Of a water that flows, With a lullaby sound,
From a spring but a very few Feet under ground—
From a cavern not very far Down under ground.
And ah! let it never Be foolishly said
That my room it is gloomy And narrow my bed;
For man never slept In a different bed—
And, to sleep, you must slumber In just such a bed.
My tantalized spirit
Here blandly reposes, Forgetting, or never
Regretting its roses— Its old agitations
Of myrtles and roses:
For now, while so quietly Lying, it fancies

A holier odor
About it, of pansies— A rosemary odor,
Commingled with pansies— With rue and the beautiful
Puritan pansies.
And so it lies happily, Bathing in many
A dream of the truth
And the beauty of Annie—
Drowned in a bath
Of the tresses of Annie.
She tenderly kissed me, She fondly caressed,
And then I fell gently
To sleep on her breast— Deeply to sleep
From the heaven of her breast.
When the light was extinguished, She covered me warm,
And she prayed to the angels To keep me from harm—
To the queen of the angels To shield me from harm.
And I lie so composedly, Now in my bed,
(Knowing her love)
That you fancy me dead— And I rest so contentedly,
Now in my bed,
(With her love at my breast) That you fancy me dead—
That you shudder to look at me, Thinking me dead:—
But my heart it is brighter Than all of the many
Stars in the sky,
For it sparkles with Annie— It glows with the light
Of the love of my Annie— With the thought of the light
Of the eyes of my Annie.
1849.

To F——

BELOVED! amid the earnest woes
That crowd around my earthly path— (Drear path, alas! where grows
Not even one lonely rose)—
My soul at least a solace hath
In dreams of thee, and therein knows An Eden of bland repose.
And thus thy memory is to me
Like some enchanted far-off isle In some tumultuos sea—
Some ocean throbbing far and free With storms—but where meanwhile
Serenest skies continually
Just o're that one bright island smile.

To Frances S. Osgood

THOU wouldst be loved?—then let thy heart From its present pathway part not!
Being everything which now thou art, Be nothing which thou art not.
So with the world thy gentle ways, Thy grace, thy more than beauty,
Shall be an endless theme of praise, And love—a simple duty.

Eldorado

Gaily bedight,
A gallant knight,
In sunshine and in shadow,
Had journeyed long,
Singing a song,
In search of Eldorado.
But he grew old—
This knight so bold—
And o'er his heart a shadow
Fell as he found
No spot of ground
That looked like Eldorado.
And, as his strength
Failed him at length,
He met a pilgrim shadow—
"Shadow," said he,
"Where can it be—
This land of Eldorado?"
"Over the mountains
Of the Moon,
Down the Valley of the Shadow,
Ride, boldly ride,"
The shade replied—
"If you seek for Eldorado!"
1849.

 Eulalie

I dwelt alone
In a world of moan,
And my soul was a stagnant tide,
Till the fair and gentle Eulalie became my blushing bride—
Till the yellow—haired young Eulalie became my smiling bride.
Ah, less—less bright
The stars of the night
Than the eyes of the radiant girl!
That the vapor can make
With the moon—tints of purple and pearl,
Can vie with the modest Eulalie's most unregarded curl—
Can compare with the bright—eyed Eulalie's most humble and careless curl.
Now Doubt—now Pain
Come never again,
For her soul gives me sigh for sigh,
And all day long
Shines, bright and strong,
Astarte within the sky,
While ever to her dear Eulalie upturns her matron eye—
While ever to her young Eulalie upturns her violet eye.
1845.

A Dream Within A Dream

Take this kiss upon the brow! And, in parting from you now,
Thus much let me avow— You are not wrong, who deem
That my days have been a dream; Yet if hope has flown away
In a night, or in a day, In a vision, or in none,
Is it therefore the less gone? All that we see or seem
Is but a dream within a dream.
I stand amid the roar
Of a surf-tormented shore, And I hold within my hand Grains
of the golden sand— How few! yet how they creep
Through my fingers to the deep, While I weep—while I weep!
O God! can I not grasp Them with a tighter clasp? O God! can
I not save
One from the pitiless wave? Is all that we see or seem But a
dream within a dream?. 1849

To Marie Louise (Shew) I

Of all who hail thy presence as the morning— Of all to whom thine absence is the night— The blotting utterly from out high heaven
The sacred sun—of all who, weeping, bless thee Hourly for hope—for life—ah! above all,
For the resurrection of deep-buried faith In Truth—in Virtue—in Humanity—
Of all who, on Despair's unhallowed bed Lying down to die, have suddenly arisen
At thy soft-murmured words, "Let there be light!" At the soft-murmured words that were fulfilled
In the seraphic glancing of thine eyes—
Of all who owe thee most—whose gratitude Nearest resembles worship—oh, remember The truest—the most fervently devoted,
And think that these weak lines are written by him— By him who, as he pens them, thrills to think
His spirit is communing with an angel's.

To Marie Louise (Shew) II

NOT long ago, the writer of these lines, In the mad pride of intellectuality,
Maintained "the power of words"—denied that ever A thought arose within the human brain
Beyond the utterance of the human tongue: And now, as if in mockery of that boast, Two words-two foreign soft
dissyllables— Italian tones, made only to be murmured By angels dreaming in the moonlit "dew
That hangs like chains of pearl on Hermon hill,"— Have stirred from out the abysses of his heart, Unthought-like thoughts that are the souls of thought, Richer, far wider, far diviner visions Than even the seraph harper, Israfel,
(Who has "the sweetest voice of all God's creatures") Could hope to utter. And I! my spells are broken.
The pen falls powerless from my shivering hand. With thy dear name as text, though bidden by thee, I can not write-I can not speak or think—
Alas, I can not feel; for 'tis not feeling, This standing motionless upon the golden
Threshold of the wide-open gate of dreams, Gazing, entranced, adown the gorgeous vista, And thrilling as I see, upon the right,
Upon the left, and all the way along, Amid empurpled vapors, far away
To where the prospect terminates-thee only!

The City In The Sea

Lo! Death has reared himself a throne In a strange city lying alone
Far down within the dim West,
Wherethe good and the bad and the worst and the best Have gone to their eternal rest.
There shrines and palaces and towers (Time-eaten towers that tremble not!) Resemble nothing that is ours.
Around, by lifting winds forgot, Resignedly beneath the sky
The melancholy waters lie.

No rays from the holy heaven come down On the long night-time of that town;
But light from out the lurid sea Streams up the turrets silently—
Gleams up the pinnacles far and free— Up domes—up spires—up kingly halls— Up fanes—up Babylon-like walls—
Up shadowy long-forgotten bowers Of sculptured ivy and stone flowers—
Up many and many a marvellous shrine Whose wreathed friezes intertwine
The viol, the violet, and the vine.

Resignedly beneath the sky The melancholy waters lie.
So blend the turrets and shadows there That all seem pendulous in air,

While from a proud tower in the town Death looks gigantically down.

There open fanes and gaping graves Yawn level with the luminous waves; But not the riches there that lie
In each idol's diamond eye— Not the gaily-jewelled dead

Tempt the waters from their bed; For no ripples curl, alas!
Along that wilderness of glass— No swellings tell that winds may be Upon some far-off happier sea—
No heavings hint that winds have been On seas less hideously serene.

But lo, a stir is in the air!
The wave—there is a movement there! As if the towers had thrown aside,
In slightly sinking, the dull tide— As if their tops had feebly given A void within the filmy Heaven.
The waves have now a redder glow— The hours are breathing faint and low— And when, amid no earthly moans, Down, down that town shall settle hence, Hell, rising from a thousand thrones, Shall do it reverence.

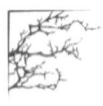 # The Sleeper

At midnight in the month of June, I stand beneath the mystic moon. An opiate vapour, dewy, dim, Exhales from out her golden rim,
And, softly dripping, drop by drop, Upon the quiet mountain top.
Steals drowsily and musically Into the univeral valley.
The rosemary nods upon the grave; The lily lolls upon the wave; Wrapping the fog about its breast, The ruin moulders into rest; Looking like Lethe, see! the lake
A conscious slumber seems to take, And would not, for the world, awake. All Beauty sleeps!—and lo! where lies (Her easement open to the skies) Irene, with her Destinies!
Oh, lady bright! can it be right— This window open to the night? The wanton airs, from the tree-top,
Laughingly through the lattice drop— The bodiless airs, a wizard rout,
Flit through thy chamber in and out, And wave the curtain canopy
So fitfully—so fearfully—
Above the closed and fringed lid
'Neath which thy slumb'ring sould lies hid, That o'er the floor and down the wall, Like ghosts the shadows rise and fall!
Oh, lady dear, hast thous no fear? Why and what art thou dreaming here? Sure thou art come p'er far-off seas,
A wonder to these garden trees! Strange is thy pallor! strange thy dress! Strange, above all, thy length of tress,
 And this all solemn silentness!
The lady sleeps! Oh, may her sleep, Which is enduring, so be deep!
Heaven have her in its sacred keep!

This chamber changed for one more holy, This bed for one more melancholy,
I pray to God that she may lie Forever with unopened eye,
While the dim sheeted ghosts go by!
My love, she sleeps! Oh, may her sleep, As it is lasting, so be deep!
Soft may the worms about her creep! Far in the forest, dim and old,
For her may some tall vault unfold— Some vault that oft hath flung its black And winged pannels fluttering back,
Triumphant, o'er the crested palls,
Of her grand family funerals— Some sepulchre, remote, alone,
Against whose portal she hath thrown, In childhood, many an idle s tone—
Some tomb fromout whose sounding door She ne'er shall force an echo more, Thrilling to think, poor child of sin!
It was the dead who groaned within.
1845.

Bridal Ballad

THE ring is on my hand,
And the wreath is on my brow; Satins and jewels grand
Are all at my command, And I am happy now.

And my lord he loves me well;
But, when first he breathed his vow, I felt my bosom swell—
For the words rang as a knell, And the voice seemed his who fell In the battle down the dell,

And who is happy now.

But he spoke to re-asure me, And he kissed my pallid brow,
While a reverie came o're me, And to the church-yard bore me, And I sighed to him before me, Thinking him dead D'Elormie,
"Oh, I am happy now!"

And thus the words were spoken, And this the plighted vow,
And, though my faith be broken, And, though my heart be broken, Behold the golden token
That proves me happy now!

Would God I could awaken!
For I dream I know not how, And my soul is sorely shaken
Lest an evil step be taken,— Lest the dead who is forsaken
May not be happy now.

Poems Of Manhood

The Coliseum

TYPE of the antique Rome! Rich reliquary Of lofty contemplation left to Time
By buried centuries of pomp and power! At length—at length—after so many days Of weary pilgrimage and burning thirst,
(Thirst for the springs of lore that in thee lie,) I kneel, an altered and an humble man,
Amid thy shadows, and so drink within
My very soul thy grandeur, gloom, and glory!
Vastness! and Age! and Memories of Eld! Silence! and Desolation! and dim Night!
I feel ye now—I feel ye in your strength— O spells more sure than e'er Judæan king Taught in the gardens of Gethsemane!
O charms more potent than the rapt Chaldee Ever drew down from out the quiet stars!
Here, where a hero fell, a column falls! Here, where the mimic eagle glared in gold, A midnight vigil holds the swarthy bat!
Here, where the dames of Rome their gilded hair Waved to the wind, now wave the reed and thistle! Here, where on golden throne the monarch lolled, Glides, spectre-like, unto his marble home,
Lit by the wanlight—wan light of the horned moon, The swift and silent lizard of the stones!
But stay! these walls—these ivy-clad arcades—
These mouldering plinths—these sad and blackened shafts—
These vague entablatures—this crumbling frieze—
These shattered cornices—this wreck—this ruin— These stones—alas! these gray stones—are they all— All of the famed, and the colossal left
By the corrosive Hours to Fate and me?
"Not all"—the Echoes answer me—"not all! "Prophetic sounds and loud, arise forever "From us, and from all Ruin, unto the wise, "As melody from Memnon to the Sun.
"We rule the hearts of mightiest men—we rule "With a despotic sway all giant minds.
"We are not impotent—we pallid stones.

"Not all our power is gone—not all our fame— "Not all the magic of our high renown—
"Not all the wonder that encircles us— "Not all the mysteries that in us lie— "Not all the memories that hang upon
"And cling around about us as a garment, "Clothing us in a robe of more than glory."

 Lenore

AH broken is the golden bowl! the spirit flown forever! Let the bell toll!—a saintly soul floats on the Stygian river;
And, Guy De Vere, hast thou no tear?—weep now or never more! See! on yon drear and rigid bier low lies thy love, Lenore!
Come! let the burial rite be read—the funeral song be sung!—
An anthem for the queenliest dead that ever died so young—
A dirge for her the doubly dead in that she died so young.
"Wretches! ye loved her for her wealth and hated her for her pride, "And when she fell in feeble health, ye blessed her—that she died! "How shall the ritual, then, be read?—the requiem how be sung "By you—by yours, the evil eye,—by yours, the slanderous tongue "That did to death the innocent that died, and died so young?"
Peccavimus; but rave not thus! and let a Sabbath song Go up to God so solemnly the dead may feel so wrong!
The sweet Lenore hath "gone before," with Hope, that flew beside Leaving thee wild for the dear child that should have been thy bride— For her, the fair and debonair, that now so lowly lies,
The life upon her yellow hair but not within her eyes—
The life still there, upon her hair—the death upon her eyes.
"Avaunt! to-night my heart is light. No dirge will I upraise,
"But waft the angel on her flight with a Paean of old days!
"Let no bell toll!—lest her sweet soul, amid its hallowed mirth,
"Should catch the note, as it doth float—up from the damned Earth. "To friends above, from fiends below, the indignant ghost is riven— "From Hell unto a high estate far up within the Heaven—

"From grief and groan, to a golden throne, beside the King of Heaven."

To One In Paradise

THOU wast all that to me, love, For which my soul did pine—
A green isle in the sea, love, A fountain and a shrine,
All wreathed with fairy fruits and flowers, And all the flowers were mine.

Ah, dream too bright to last!
Ah, starry Hope! that didst arise But to be overcast!
A voice from out the Future cries, "On! on!"—but o'er the Past
(Dim gulf!) my spirit hovering lies Mute, motionless, aghast!

For, alas! alas! with me The light of Life is o'er!
No more—no more—no more— (Such language holds the solemn sea
To the sands upon the shore) Shall bloom the thunder-blasted tree,
Or the stricken eagle soar!

And all my days are trances, And all my nightly dreams
Are where thy dark eye glances, And where thy footstep gleams—
In what ethereal dances, By what eternal streams.
1835.

 The Haunted Palace

IN the greenest of our valleys By good angels tenanted,
Once a fair and stately palace— Radiant palace—reared its head.
In the monarch Thought's dominion— It stood there!
Never seraph spread a pinion Over fabric half so fair.
Banners yellow, glorious, golden, On its roof did float and flow,
(This—all this—was in the olden Time long ago,)
And every gentle air that dallied, In that sweet day,
Along the ramparts plumed and pallid, A winged odour went away.
Wanderers in that happy valley, Through two luminous windows, saw
Spirits moving musically,
To a lute's well-tuned law,
Round about a throne where, sitting (Porphyrogene)
In state his glory well befitting,
The ruler of the realm was seen.
And all with pearl and ruby glowing Was the fair palace door,
Through which came flowing, flowing, flowing, And sparkling evermore,
A troop of Echoes, whose sweet duty Was but to sing,
In voices of surpassing beauty,
The wit and wisdom of their king.
But evil things, in robes of sorrow,
Assailed the monarch's high estate. (Ah, let us mourn!—for never sorrow
Shall dawn upon him desolate!) And round about his home the glory
That blushed and bloomed, Is but a dim-remembered story
Of the old time entombed.

And travellers, now, within that valley, Through the red-litten windows see
Vast forms, that move fantastically To a discordant melody,
While, lie a ghastly rapid river, Through the pale door
A hideous throng rush out forever And laugh—but smile no more.

The Conqueror Worm

Lo! 'tis a gala night
Within the lonesome latter years! An angel throng, bewinged, bedight
In veils, and drowned in tears, Sit in a theatre, to see
A play of hopes and fears,
While the orchestra breathes fitfully The music of the spheres.
Mimes, in the form of God on high, Mutter and mumble low,
And hither and thither fly—
Mere puppets they, who come and go At bidding of vast formless things
That shift the scenery to and fro, Flapping from out their Condor wings
Invisible Wo!
That motley drama—oh, be sure It shall not be forgot!
With its Phantom chased for evermore, By a crowd that seize it not,
Through a circle that ever returneth in To the self-same spot,
And much of Ma dness, and more of Sin, And Horror the soul of the plot.
But see, amid the mimic rout A crawling shape intrude!
A blood-red thing that writhes from out The scenic solitude!
It writhes!—it writhes!—with mortal pangs The mimes become its food,
And the angels sob at vermin fangs In human gore imbued.
Out—out are the lights—out all!
 And, over each quivering form, The curtain, a funeral pall,
Comes down with the rush of a storm, And the angels, all pallid and wan,
Uprising, unveiling, affirm
That the play is the tragedy, "Man," And its hero the Conqueror Worm.

Silence

THERE are some qualities—some incorporate things, That have a double life, which thus is made
A type of that twin entity which springs
From matter and light, evinced in solid and shade.
There is a two-fold Silence—sea and shore— Body and soul. One dwells in lonely places,
Newly with grass o'ergrown; some solemn graces, Some human memories and tearful lore,
Render him terrorless: his name's "No More." He is the corporate Silence: dread him not!
No power hath he of evil in himself;
But should some urgent fate (untimely lot!) Bring thee to meet his shadow (nameless elf,
That haunteth the lone regions where hath trod No foot of man,) commend thyself to God!

Dream-Land

BY a route obscure and lonely, Haunted by ill angels only,
Where an Eidolon, named NIGHT, On a black throne reigns upright,
I have reached these lands but newly From an ultimate dim Thule—
From a wild weird clime that lieth, sublime, Out of SPACE—out of TIME.
Bottomless vales and boundless floods, And chasms, and caves, and Titian woods, With forms that no man can discover
For the dews that drip all over; Mountains toppling evermore Into seas without a shore; Seas that restlessly aspire, Surging, unto skies of fire; Lakes that endlessly outspread
Their lone waters—lone and dead,— Their still waters—still and chilly With the snows of the lolling lily.
By the lakes that thus outspread Their lone waters, lone and dead,— Their sad waters, sad and chilly With the snows of the lolling lily,— By the mountains—near the river Murmuring lowly, murmuring ever,— By the grey woods,—by the swamp Where the toad and the newt encamp,— By the dismal tarns and pools
Where dwell the Ghouls,— By each spot the most unholy— In each nook most melancholy,— There the traveller meets aghast Sheeted Memories of the Past—
Shrouded forms that start and sigh
As they pass the wanderer by—
White-robed forms of friends long given, In agony, to the Earth—and Heaven.
For the heart whose woes are legion 'Tis a peaceful, soothing region— For the spirit that walks in shadow 'Tis—oh 'tis an Eldorado!
But the traveller, travelling through it, May not—dare not openly view it; Never its mysteries are exposed
To the weak human eye unclosed; So wills its King, who hath forbid The uplifting of the fringed lid;
And thus the sad Soul that here passes Beholds it but through darkened glasses.

By a route obscure and lonely, Haunted by ill angels only, Where an Eidolon, named NIGHT, On a black throne reigns upright, I have wandered home but newly From this ultimate dim Thule.

Hymn

AT morn—at noon—at twilight dim— Maria! thou hast heard my hymn!
In joy and wo—in good and ill— Mother of God, be with me still! When the Hours flew brightly by And not a cloud obscured the sky, My soul, lest it should truant be,
Thy grace did guide to thine and thee; Now, when storms of Fate o'ercast Darkly my Present and my Past,
Let my Future radiant shine
With sweet hopes of thee and thine!

To Zante

FAIR isle, that from the fairest of all flowers, Thy gentlest of all gentle names dost take
How many memories of what radiant hours At sight of thee and thine at once awake!
How many scenes of what departed bliss!
How many thoughts of what entombed hopes!
How many visions of a maiden that is
No more—no more upon thy verdant slopes!
No more! alas, that magical sad sound
Transfomring all! Thy charms shall please no more— Thy memory no more! Accursed ground
Henceforth I hold thy flower-enamelled shore, O hyacinthine isle! O purple Zante!
"Isoa d'oro! Fior di Levante!"

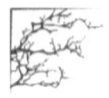 Scenes From "Politian"

AN UNPUBLISHED DRAMA.
I.
ROME.—A Hall in a Palace Alessandra and Castiglione.
Alessandra. Thou art sad, Castiglione. Castiglione. Sad!—not I.
Oh, I'm the happiest, happiest man in Rome!
A few days more, thou knowest, my Alessandra, Will make thee mine. Oh, I am very happy!
Aless. Methinks thou hast a singular way of showing Thy happiness!—what ails thee, cousin of mine?
Why didst thou sigh so deeply?
Cas. Did I sign?
I was not conscious of it. It is a fashion, A silly—a most silly fashion I have
When I am very happy. Did I sigh?   (sighing.)
Aless. Thou didst. Thou art not well. Thou hast indulged Too much of late, and I am vexed to see it.
Late hours and wine, Castiglione,—these Will ruin thee! thou art already altered—
Thy looks are haggard—nothing so wears away The constitution as late hours and wine.
Cas. (musing.) Nothing, fair cousin, nothing—not even deep sorrow—
Wears it away like evil hours and wine. I will amend.
Aless. Do it! I would have thee drop
Thy riotous company, too—fellows low born—
Ill suit the like with old Di Broglio's heir And Alessandra's husband.
Cas. I will drop them.
Aless. Thou wilt—thou must. Attend thou also more To thy dress and equipage—they are over plain
For thy lofty rank and fashion—much depends Upon appearances.

Cas. I'll see to it.
Aless. Then see to it!—pay more attention, sir, To a becoming carriage—much thou wantest
In dignity.
Cas. Much, much, oh! much I want In proper dignity.
Aless.(haughtily) Thou mockest me, sir! Cas. (abstractedly.) Sweet, gentle Lalage! Aless. Heard I aright?
I speak to him—he speaks of Lalage!
Sir Count! (places her hand on his shoulder) what art thou dreaming? he's not well!
What ails thee, sir?
Cas. (startling.) Cousin! fair cousin!—madam!
I crave thy pardon—indeed I am not well— Your hand from off my shoulder, if you please.
This air is most oppressive!—Madam—the Duke!
Enter Di Broglio.
Di Broglio. My son, I've news for thee!—hey?—what's the matter? (observing Alessandra)
I' the pouts? Kiss her, Castiglione! kiss her, You dog! and make it up, I say, this minute! I've news for you both. Politian is expected Hourly in Rome—Politian, Earl of Leicester! We'll have him at the wedding. 'Tis his first visit
To the imperial city.
Aless. What! Politian
Of Britain, Earl of Leicester?
Di Brog. The same, my love.
We'll have him at the wedding. A man quite young In years, but grey in fame. I have not seen him, But Rumour speaks of him as of a prodigy
Pre-eminent in arts and arms, and wealth,
And high descent. We'll have him at the wedding.
Aless. I have heard much of this Politian.
Gay, volatile and giddy—is he not? And little given to thinking.
Di Brog. Far from it, love.
No branch, they say, of all philosophy
So deep abstruse he has not mastered it. Learned as few are learned.
Aless. 'Tis very strange!
I have known men have seen Politian

And sought his company. They speak of him As of one who entered madly into life, Drinking the cup of pleasure to the dregs.
Cas. Ridiculous! Now I have seen Politian And know him well—nor learned nor mirthful he. He is a dreamer and a man shut out
From common passions.
Di Brog. Children, we disagree.
Let us go forth and taste the fragrant air Of the garden. Did I dream, or did I hear
Politian was a melancholy man?   (exeunt.)
II
ROME. A Lady's apartment, with a window open and looking into a garden. Lalage, in deep mourning, reading at a table on which lie some books and a hand mirror. In the background Jacinta (a servant maid) leans carelessly upon a chair.
Lal. [Lalage] Jacinta! is it thou?
Jac. [Jacinta] (pertly.) Yes, Ma'am, I'm here.
Lal.   I did not know, Jacinta, you were in waiting.
Sit down!—Let not my presence trouble you— Sit down!—for I am humble, most humble.
Jac. (aside.) 'Tis time.
(Jacinta seats herself in a side-long manner upon the chair, resting her elbows upon the back, and regarding her mistress with a contemptuous look. Lalage continues to read.)
Lal. "It in another climate, so he said,
"Bore a bright golden flower, but not i' this soil!" (pauses—turns over some leaves, and resumes) "No lingering winters there, nor snow, nor shower— "But Ocean ever to refresh mankind "Breathes the shrill spirit of the western wind." O, beautiful!—most beautiful—how like
To what my fevered soul doth dream of Heaven!
O happy land (pauses) She died!—the maiden died! A still more happy maiden who couldst die!
Jacinta!
(Jacinta returns no answer, and Lalage presently resumes.)
Again!—a similar tale
Told of a beauteous dame beyond the sea!
Thus speaketh one Ferdinand in the words of the play— "She died full young"—one Bossola answers him—

"I think not so—her infelicity
"Seemed to have years too many"—Ah luckless lady! Jacinta!
(still no answer)
Here's a far sterner story,
But like—oh, very like in its despair—
Of that Egyptian queen, winning so easily
A thousand hearts—losing at length her own.
She died. Thus endeth the history—and her maids Lean over and weep —two gentle maids
With gentle names—Eiros and Charmion! Rainbow and Dove!——Jacinta!
Jac. (pettishly.) Madam, what is it?
Lal. Wilt thou, my good Jacinta, be so kind As go down in the library and bring me
The Holy Evangelists.
Jac. Pshaw!   (exit.) Lal. If there be balm
For the wounded spirit in Gilead it is there! Dew in the night time of my bitter trouble
Will there be found—"dew sweeter far than that Which hangs like chains of pearl on Hermon hill."
(re-enter Jacinta, and throws a volume on the table.)
There, ma'am, 's the book. Indeed she is very troublesome.
(aside.)
Lal. (astonished.) What didst thou say, Jacinta? Have I done aught To grieve thee or to vex thee?—I am sorry.
For thou hast served me long and ever been
Trust-worthy and respectful.   (resumes her reading.)
Jac. I can't believe
She has any more jewels—no—no—she gave me all. (aside.)
Lal. What didst thou say, Jacinta? Now I bethink me Thou hast not spoken lately of thy wedding.
How fares good Ugo?—and when is it to be? Can I do aught?—is there no farther aid Thou needest, Jacinta?
Jac. Is there no farther aid!
That's meant for me. (aside) I'm sure, madam, you need not Be always throwing those jewels in my teeth.
Lal. Jewels! Jacinta,—now indeed, Jacinta, I thought not of the jewels.
Jac. Oh! perhaps not!
But then I might have sworn it. After all, There's Ugo says the ring is only paste, For he's sure the Count Castiglione never

Would have given a real diamond to such as you; And at the best I'm certain, Madam, you cannot
Have use for jewels now. But I might have sworn it.   (exit.)
(Lalage bursts into tears and leans her head upon the table—after a short pause raises it.)
Lal. Poor Lalage!—and is it come to this?
Thy servant maid!—but courage!—'tis but a viper Whom thou hast cherished to sting thee to the soul! (taking up the mirror) Ha! here at least 's a friend—too much a friend In earlier days—a friend will not deceive thee. Fair mirror and true! now tell me (for thou canst) A tale—a pretty tale—and heed thou not Though it be rife with woe: It answers me.
It speaks of sunken eyes, and wasted cheeks, And Beauty long deceased—remembers me Of Joy departed—Hope, the Seraph Hope, Inurned and entombed:—now, in a tone
Low, sad, and solemn, but most audible, Whispers of early grave untimely yawning
For ruined maid. Fair mirror and true—thou liest not! Thou hast no end to gain—no heart to break— Castiglione lied who said he loved—
Thou true—he false!—false!—false!
(While she speaks, a monk enters her apartment, and approaches unobserved.)
Monk. Refuge thou hast,
Sweet daughter, in Heaven. Think of eternal things! Give up thy soul to penitence, and pray!
Lal. (arising hurriedly.) I cannot pray!—My soul is at war with God!
The frightful sounds of merriment below Disturb my senses—go! I cannot pray— The sweet airs from the garden worry me!
Thy presence grieves me—go!—thy priestly raiment Fills me with dread—thy ebony crucifix
With horror and awe!
Monk. Think of thy precious soul!
Lal. Think of my early days!—think of my father And mother in Heaven think of our quiet home,
 And the rivulet that ran before the door! Think of my little sisters!—think of them! And think of me!—think of my trusting love
And confidence—his vows—my ruin—think—think Of my unspeakable misery!—begone!

Yet stay! yet stay!—what was it thou saidst of prayer And penitence? Didst thou not speak of faith
And vows before the throne?
Monk. I did.
Lal. Lal. 'Tis well.
There is a vow were fitting should be made— A sacred vow, imperative, and urgent,
A solemn vow!
Monk. Daughter, this zeal is well!
Lal. Father, this zeal is anything but well!
Hast thou a crucifix fit for this thing? A crucifix whereon to register
This sacred vow?   (he hands her his own) Not that—Oh! no!—no!—no!   (shuddering) Not that! Not that!—I tell thee, holy man,
Thy raiments and thy ebony cross affright me! Stand back! I have a crucifix myself,—
I have a crucifix Methinks 'twere fitting
The deed—the vow—the symbol of the deed— And the deed's register should tally, father!
(draws a cross-handled dagger, and raises it on high) Behold the cross wherewith a vow like mine
Is written in Heaven!
Monk. Thy words are madness, daughter, And speak a purpose unholy—thy lips are livid— Thine eyes are wild— tempt not the wrath divine! Pause ere too late!—oh, be not—be not rash!
Swear not the oath—oh, swear it not!
Lal. 'Tis sworn!
III.
An apartment in a Palace. Politian and Baldazzar.
Baldazzar.———Arouse thee now, Politian!
Thou must not—nay indeed, indeed, shalt not Give away unto these humors. Be thyself!
Shake off the idle fancies that beset thee, And live, for now thou diest!
Politian. Not so, Baldazzar! Surely I live. Bal. Politian, it doth grieve me
To see thee thus.
Pol. Baldazzar, it doth grieve me

To give thee cause for grief, my honoured friend. Command
me, sir! what wouldst thou have me do? At thy behest I will
shake off that nature
Which from my, forefathers I did inherit, Which with my
mother's milk I did imbibe, And be no more Politian, but some
other. Command me, sir!
Bal. To the field, then—to the field— To the senate or the field.
Pol. Alas! Alas!
There is an imp would follow me even there! There is an imp
hath followed me even there! There is—what voice was that?
Bal. I heard it not.
I heard not any voice except thine own, And the echo of thine
own.
Pol. Then I but dreamed.
Bal. Give not thy soul to dreams: the camp—the court, Befit
thee—Fame awaits thee—Glory calls—
And her the trumpet-tongued thou wilt not hear In hearkening
to imaginary sounds
And phantom voices.
Pol. It is a phantom voice!
Didst thou not hear it then?
Bal. I heard it not.
Pol. Thou heardst it not!—Baldazaar, speak no more To me,
Politian, of thy camps and courts.
Oh! I am sick, sick, sick, even unto death, Of the hollow and
high-sounding vanities
Of the populous Earth! Bear with me yet awhile! We have
been boys together—schoolfellows— And now are friends—yet
shall not be so long— For in the eternal city thou shalt do me
A kind and gentle office, and a Power—
A Power august, benignant and supreme— Shall then absolve
thee of all further duties Unto thy friend.
Bal. Thou speakest a fearful riddle I will not understand.
Pol. Yet now as Fate
Approaches, and the Hours are breathing low, The sands of
Time are changed to golden grains, And dazzle me, Baldazzar.
Alas! alas!
I cannot die, having within my heart So keen a relish for the
beautiful
As hath been kindled within it. Methinks the air Is balmier
now than it was wont to be—

Rich melodies are floating in the winds— A rarer loveliness bedecks the earth— And with a holier lustre the quiet moon Sitteth in Heaven.—Hist! hist! thou canst not say Thou hearest not now, Baldazzar?
Bal. Indeed I hear not.
Pol. Not hear it!—listen now!—listen!—the faintest sound And yet the sweetest that ear ever heard!
A lady's voice!—and sorrow in the tone! Baldazzar, it oppresses me like a spell! Again!—again!—how solemnly it falls
Into my heart of hearts! that eloquent voice
Surely I never heard—yet it were well Had I but heard it with its thrilling tones In earlier days!
Bal. I myself hear it now.
Be still!—the voice, if I mistake not greatly, Proceeds from yonder lattice—which you may see Very plainly through the window—it belongs,
Does it not? unto this palace of the Duke. The singer is undoubtedly beneath
The roof of his Excellency—and perhaps Is even that Alessandra of whom he spoke As the betrothed of Castiglione, His son and heir.
Pol. Be still!—it comes again!
Voice "And is thy heart so strong (very faintly)   As for to leave me thus
Who hath loved thee so long
In wealth and woe among? And is thy heart so strong As for to leave me thus?
Say nay—say nay!"
Bal. The song is English, and I oft have heard it In merry England—never so plaintively—
Hist! hist! it comes again!
Voice "Is it so strong
(more loudly) As for to leave me thus Who hath loved thee so long In wealth and woe among?
And is thy heart so strong As for to leave me thus?
Say nay—say nay!"
Bal. 'Tis hushed and all is still! Pol. All is not still!
Bal. Let us go down.
Pol. Go down, Baldazzar, go!
Bal. The hour is growing late—the Duke awaits use— Thy presence is expected in the hall

Below. What ails thee, Earl Politian?
Voice "Who hath loved thee so long (distinctly) In wealth and woe among,
And is thy heart so strong?
Say nay—say nay!"
Bal. Let us descend!—'tis time. Politian, give These fancies to the wind. Remember, pray, Your bearing lately savored much of rudeness Unto the Duke. Arouse thee! and remember
Pol. Remember? I do. Lead on! I do remember.
(going.) Let us descend. Believe me I would give,
Freely would give the broad lands of my earldom To look upon the face hidden by yon lattice—
"To gaze upon that veiled face, and hear Once more that silent tongue."
Bal. Let me beg you, sir,
Descend with me—the Duke may be offended. Let us go down, I pray you.
(Voice loudly) Say nay!—say nay!
Pol. (aside) 'Tis strange!—'tis very strange—methought the voice Chimed in with my desires, and bade me stay!
(approaching the window.) Sweet voice! I heed thee, and will surely stay.
Now be this Fancy, by Heaven, or be it Fate, Still will I not descend. Baldazzar, make Apology unto the Duke for me;
I go not down to-night.
Bal. Your lordship's pleasure
Shall be attended to. Good-night, Politian.
Pol. Good-night, my friend, good-night.
IV.
The gardens of a Palace—Moonlight Lalage and Politian.
Lalge. And dost thou speak of love
To me, Politian?—dost thou speak of love To Lalage?—ah, woe—ah, woe is me!
This mockery is most cruel—most cruel indeed!
Politian. Weep not! oh, sob not thus!—thy bitter tears Will madden me. Oh, mourn not, Lalage—
Be comforted! I know—I know it all,
And still I speak of love. Look at me, brightest And beautiful Lalage!—turn here thine eyes!
Thou askest me if I could speak of love,

Knowing what I know, and seeing what I have seen. Thou askest me that—and thus I answer thee—
Thus on my bended knee I answer thee. (kneeling.) Sweet Lalage, I love thee—love thee—love thee;
Thro' good and ill—thro' weal and wo I love thee. Not mother, with her first-born on her knee, Thrills with intenser love than I for thee.
Not on God's altar, in any time or clime, Burned there a holier fire than burneth now
Within my spirit for thee. And do I love? (arising.) Even for thy woes I love thee—even for thy woes-
Thy beauty and thy woes.
Lal. Alas, proud Earl,
Thou dost forget thyself, remembering me! How, in thy father's halls, among the maidens Pure and reproachless of thy princely line, Could the dishonored Lalage abide?
Thy wife, and with a tainted memory-
MY seared and blighted name, how would it tally With the ancestral honors of thy house,
And with thy glory?
Pol. Speak not to me of glory!
I hate—I loathe the name; I do abhor The unsatisfactory and ideal thing.
Art thou not Lalage and I Politian? Do I not love—art thou not beautiful-
What need we more? Ha! glory!—now speak not of it. By all I hold most sacred and most solemn-
By all my wishes now—my fears hereafter- By all I scorn on earth and hope in heaven- There is no deed I would more glory in, Than in thy cause to scoff at this same glory And trample it under foot. What matters it- What matters it, my fairest, and my best, That we go down unhonored and forgotten Into the dust—so we descend together.
Descend together—and then—and then, perchance-
Lal. Why dost thou pause, Politian? Pol. And then, perchance Arise together, Lalage, and roam
The starry and quiet dwellings of the blest, And still-
Lal. Why dost thou pause, Politian? Pol. And still together— together.
Lal. Now Earl of Leicester!

Thou lovest me, and in my heart of hearts I feel thou lovest me truly.
Pol. Oh, Lalage!
(throwing himself upon his knee.)
And lovest thou me?
Lal. Hist! hush! within the gloom
Of yonder trees methought a figure passed-
A spectral figure, solemn, and slow, and noiseless-
Like the grim shadow Conscience, solemn and noiseless.
(walks across and returns.) I was mistaken—'twas but a giant bough
Stirred by the autumn wind. Politian!
Pol. My Lalage—my love! why art thou moved? Why dost thou turn so pale? Not Conscience' self, Far less a shadow which thou likenest to it,
Should shake the firm spirit thus. But the night wind Is chilly—and these melancholy boughs
Throw over all things a gloom.
Lal. Politian!
Thou speakest to me of love. Knowest thou the land With which all tongues are busy—a land new found— Miraculously found by one of Genoa—
A thousand leagues within the golden west?
A fairy land of flowers, and fruit, and sunshine, And crystal lakes, and over-arching forests,
And mountains, around whose towering summits the winds Of Heaven untrammelled flow—which air to breathe
Is Happiness now, and will be Freedom hereafter In days that are to come?
Pol. O, wilt thou—wilt thou
Fly to that Paradise—my Lalage, wilt thou
Fly thither with me? There Care shall be forgotten, And Sorrow shall be no more, and Eros be all.
And life shall then be mine, for I will live
For thee, and in thine eyes—and thou shalt be No more a mourner—but the radiant Joys Shall wait upon thee, and the angel Hope Attend thee ever; and I will kneel to thee
And worship thee, and call thee my beloved, My own, my beautiful, my love, my wife,
My all;—oh, wilt thou—wilt thou, Lalage, Fly thither with me?
Lal. A deed is to be done— Castiglione lives!

Pol. And he shall die!(exit)
Lal. (after a pause.) And—he—shall—die!—alas!
Castiglione die? Who spoke the words? Where am I?—what was it he said?—Politian! Thou art not gone—thou are not gone, Politian! I feel thou art not gone—yet dare not look, Lest I behold thee not; thou couldst not go
With those words upon thy lips—O, speak to me! And let me hear thy voice—one word—one word, To say thou art not gone,—one little sentence,
To say how thou dost scorn—how thou dost hate My womanly weakness. Ha! ha! thou art not gone- O speak to me! I knew thou wouldst not go!
I knew thou wouldst not, couldst not, durst not go. Villain, thou art not gone—thou mockest me!
And thus I clutch thee—thus!—He is gone, he is gone Gone—gone. Where am I?—'tis well—'tis very well! So that the blade be keen—the blow be sure,
'Tis well, 'tis very well—alas! alas!
V.
The suburbs. Politian alone.
Politian. This weakness grows upon me. I am faint, And much I fear me ill—it will not do
To die ere I have lived!—Stay, stay thy hand, O Azrael, yet awhile!—Prince of the Powers Of Darkness and the Tomb, O pity me!
O pity me! let me not perish now,
In the budding of my Paradisal Hope! Give me to live yet—yet a little while:
'Tis I who pray for life—I who so late Demanded but to die!—what sayeth the Count?
Enter Baldazzar.
Baldazzar. That knowing no cause of quarrel or of feud
Between the Earl Politian and himself.
He doth decline your cartel.
Pol. What didst thou say?
What answer was it you brought me, good Baldazzar? With what excessive fragrance the zephyr comes
 Laden fro m yonder bowers!—a fairer day, Or one more worthy Italy, methinks
No mortal eyes have seen!—what said the Count?

Bal. That he, Castiglione' not being aware Of any feud existing, or any cause
Of quarrel between your lordship and himself, Cannot accept the challenge.
Pol. It is most true—
All this is very true. When saw you, sir, When saw you now, Baldazzar, in the frigid Ungenial Britain which we left so lately,
A heaven so calm as this—so utterly free From the evil taint of clouds?—and he did say?
Bal. No more, my lord, than I have told you, sir: The Count Castiglione will not fight,
Having no cause for quarrel.
Pol. Now this is true-
All very true. Thou art my friend, Baldazzar, And I have not forgotten it—thou'lt do me
A piece of service; wilt thou go back and say Unto this man, that I, the Earl of Leicester, Hold him a villain?—thus much, I prythee, say Unto the Count—it is exceeding just
He should have cause for quarrel.
Bal. My lord!—my friend!-
Pol. (aside.) 'Tis he!—he comes himself? (aloud) Thou reasonest well.
I know what thou wouldst say—not send the message- Well!—I will think of it—I will not send it.
Now prythee, leave me—hither doth come a person With whom affairs of a most private nature
I would adjust.
Bal. I go—to-morrow we meet, Do we not?—at the Vatican.
Pol. At the Vatican. (exit Bal.)
Enter Castigilone.
Cas. The Earl of Leicester here!
Pol. I am the Earl of Leicester, and thou seest, Dost thou not? that I am here.
Cas. My lord, some strange,
Some singular mistake—misunderstanding— Hath without doubt arisen: thou hast been urged Thereby, in heat of anger, to address
Some words most unaccountable, in writing, To me,
Castiglione; the bearer being Baldazzar, Duke of Surrey. I am aware

64

Of nothing which might warrant thee in this thing, Having given thee no offence. Ha!—am I right? 'Twas a mistake?—undoubtedly—we all
Do err at times.
Pol. Draw, villain, and prate no more!
Cas. Ha!—draw?—and villain? have at thee then at once, Proud Earl!   (draws.)
Pol. (drawing.) Thus to the expiatory tomb, Untimely sepulchre, I do devote thee
In the name of Lalage!
Cas. (letting fall his sword and recoiling to the extremity of the stage)
Of Lalage!
Hold off—thy sacred hand!—avaunt, I say! Avaunt—I will not fight thee—indeed I dare not.
Pol. Thou wilt not fight with me didst say, Sir Count? Shall I be baffled thus?—now this is well; Didst say thou darest not? Ha!
Cas. I dare not—dare not—
Hold off thy hand—with that beloved name
So fresh upon thy lips I will not fight thee— I cannot—dare not.
Pol. Now by my halidom
I do believe thee!—coward, I do believe thee!
Cas. Ha!—coward!—this may not be!
(clutches his sword and staggers towards POLITIAN, but his purpose is changed before reaching him, and he falls upon his knee at the feet of the Earl)
Alas! my lord,
It is—it is—most true. In such a cause I am the veriest coward. O pity me!
Pol. (greatly softened.) Alas!—I do—indeed I pity thee. Cas. And Lalage-
Pol. Scoundrel!—arise and die!
Cas. It needeth not be—thus—thus—O let me die Thus on my bended knee. It were most fitting
That in this deep humiliation I perish. For in the fight I will not raise a hand
Against thee, Earl of Leicester. Strike thou home—
(baring his bosom.) Here is no let or hindrance to thy weapon- Strike home. I will not fight thee.
Pol. Now, s' Death and Hell!

Am I not—am I not sorely—grievously tempted To take thee at thy word? But mark me, sir, Think not to fly me thus. Do thou prepare
For public insult in the streets—before The eyes of the citizens. I'll follow thee Like an avenging spirit I'll follow thee
Even unto death. Before those whom thou lovest- Before all Rome I'll taunt thee, villain,—I'll taunt thee, Dost hear? with cowardice—thou wilt not fight me?
Thou liest! thou shalt!   (exit.)
Cas. Now this indeed is just!
Most righteous, and most just, avenging Heaven!
{In the book there is a gap in numbering the notes between 12 and 29.
—ED}
NOTE
29. Such portions of "Politian" as are known to the public first saw the light of publicity in the "Southern Literary Messenger" for December, 1835, and January, 1836, being styled "Scenes from Politian: an unpublished drama." These scenes were included, unaltered, in the 1845 collection of Poems, by Poe. The larger portion of the original draft subsequently became the property of the present editor, but it is not considered just to the poet's memory to publish it. The work is a hasty and unrevised production of its author's earlier days of literary labor; and, beyond the scenes already known, scarcely calculated to enhance his reputation. As a specimen, however, of the parts unpublished, the following fragment from the first scene of Act II. may be offered. The Duke, it should be premised, is uncle to Alessandra, and father of Castiglione her betrothed.
Duke. Why do you laugh? Castiglione. Indeed
I hardly know myself. Stay! Was it not
On yesterday we were speaking of the Earl? Of the Earl Politian? Yes! it was yesterday.
Alessandra, you and I, you must remember! We were walking in the garden.
Duke, Perfectly.
I do remember it-what of it-what then?
Cas. O nothing-nothing at all. Duke. Nothing at all!
It is most singular that you should laugh 'At nothing at all!
Cas. Most singular-singular!

Duke. Look you, Castiglione, be so kind As tell me, sir, at once what 'tis you mean. What are you talking of?
Cas. Was it not so?
We differed in opinion touching him.
Duke. Him!—Whom?
Cas. Why, sir, the Earl Politian.
Duke. The Earl of Leicester! Yes!—is it he you mean?
We differed, indeed. If I now recollect
The words you used were that the Earl you knew Was neither learned nor mirthful.
Cas. Ha! ha!—now did I?
Duke. That did you, sir, and well I knew at the time You were wrong, it being not the character
Of the Earl-whom all the world allows to be A most hilarious man. Be not, my son,
Too positive again.
Cas. 'Tis singular!
Most singular! I could not think it possible So little time could so much alter one!
To say the truth about an hour ago,
As I was walking with the Count San Ozzo, All arm in arm, we met this very man
The Earl-he, with his friend Baldazzar,
Having just arrived in Rome. Ha! ha! he is altered! Such an account he gave me of his journey!
'Twould have made you die with laughter-such tales he told
Of his caprices and his merry freaks
Along the road-such oddity-such humor—
Such wit-such whim-such flashes of wild merriment Set off too in such full relief by the grave Demeanor of his friend-who, to speak the truth, Was gravity itself—
Duke. Did I not tell you?
Cas. You did-and yet 'tis strange! but true as strange, How much I was mistaken! I always thought
The Earl a gloomy man.
Duke. So, so, you see! Be not too positive. Whom have we here?
It can not be the Earl?
Cas. The Earl! Oh, no! 'Tis not the Earl-but yet it is-and leaning Upon his friend Baldazzar. AM welcome, sir!
(Enter Politian and Baldazzar.)

My lord, a second welcome let me give you To Rome-his Grace the Duke of Broglio.
Father! this is the Earl Politian, Earl
Of Leicester in Great Britain. [Politian bows haughtily.] That, his friend
Baldazzar, Duke of Surrey. The Earl has letters, So please you, for Your Grace.
Duke. Ha! ha! Most welcome
To Rome and to our palace, Earl Politian!
And you, most noble Duke! I am glad to see you! I knew your father well, my Lord Politian.
Castiglione! call your cousin hither,
And let me make the noble Earl acquainted With your betrothed. You come, sir, at a time Most seasonable. The wedding—
Politian. Touching those letters, sir,
Your son made mention of—your son, is he not? Touching those letters, sir, I wot not of them.
If such there be, my friend Baldazzar here— Baldazzar! ah!— my friend Baldazzar here Will hand them to Your Grace. I would retire.
Duke. Retire!—So soon?
Came What ho! Benito! Rupert!
His lordship's chambers-show his lordship to them! His lordship is unwell.   (Enter Benito.)
Ben. This way, my lord! (Exit, followed by Politian.) Duke. Retire! Unwell!
Bal. So please you, sir. I fear me 'Tis as you say—his lordship is unwell. The damp air of the evening-the fatigue
Of a long journey—the—indeed I had better Follow his lordship. He must be unwell.
I will return anon.
Duke. Return anon!
Now this is very strange! Castiglione!
This way, my son, I wish to speak with thee. You surely were mistaken in what you said
Of the Earl, mirthful, indeed!—which of us said Politian was a melancholy man?   (Exeunt.)

Poems Of Youth

Sonnet—To Science

SCIENCE! true daughter of Old Time thou art!
Who alterest all things with thy peering eyes.
Why preyest thou thus upon the poet's heart, Vulture, whose wings are dull realities?
How should he love thee? or how deem thee wise, Who wouldst not leave him in his wandering
To seek for treasure in the jewelled skies Albeit he soared with an undaunted wing?
Hast thou not dragged Diana from her car? And driven the Hamadryad from the wood
To seek a shelter in some happier star?
Hast thous not torn the Naiad from her flood, The Elfin from the green grass, and from me
The summer dream beneath the tamarind tree?

 Letter To Mr. B—

"WEST POINT, 1831.
"Dear B......... Believing only a portion of my former volume to be worthy a second edition-that small portion I thought it as well to include in the present book as to republish by itself. I have therefore herein combined 'Al Aaraaf' and 'Tamerlane' with other poems hitherto unprinted. Nor have I hesitated to insert from the 'Minor Poems,' now omitted, whole lines, and even passages, to the end that being placed in a fairer light, and the trash shaken from them in which they were imbedded, they may have some chance of being seen by posterity.
"It has been said that a good critique on a poem may be written by one who is no poet himself. This, according to your idea and mine of poetry, I feel to be false-the less poetical the critic, the less just the critique, and the converse. On this account, and because there are but few B-'s in the world, I would be as much ashamed of the world's good opinion as proud of your own. Another than yourself might here observe, 'Shakespeare is in possession of the world's good opinion, and yet Shakespeare is the greatest of poets. It appears then that the world judge correctly, why should you be ashamed of their favorable judgment?' The difficulty lies in the interpretation of the word 'judgment' or 'opinion.' The opinion is the world's, truly, but it may be called theirs as a man would call a book

his, having bought it; he did not write the book, but it is his; they did not originate the opinion, but it is theirs. A fool, for example, thinks Shakespeare a great poet-yet the fool has never read Shakespeare. But the fool's neighbor, who is a step higher on the Andes of the mind, whose head (that is to say, his more exalted thought) is too far above the fool to be seen or understood, but whose feet (by which I mean his everyday actions) are sufficiently near to be discerned, and by means of which that superiority is ascertained, which but for them would never have been discovered-this neighbor asserts that Shakespeare is a great poet—the fool believes him, and it is henceforward his opinion. This neighbor's own opinion has, in like manner, been adopted from one above him, and so, ascendingly, to a few gifted individuals who kneel around the summit, beholding, face to face, the master spirit who stands upon the pinnacle.

"You are aware of the great barrier in the path of an American writer. He is read, if at all, in preference to the combined and established wit of the world. I say established; for it is with literature as with law or empire-an established name is an estate in tenure, or a throne in possession. Besides, one might suppose that books, like their authors, improve by travel-their having crossed the sea is, with us, so great a distinction. Our antiquaries abandon time for distance; our very fops glance from the binding to the bottom of the title-page, where the mystic characters which spell London, Paris, or Genoa, are precisely so many letters of recommendation.

"I mentioned just now a vulgar error as regards criticism. I think the notion that no poet can form a correct estimate of his own writings is another. I remarked before that in proportion to the poetical talent would be the justice of a critique upon poetry. Therefore a bad poet would, I grant, make a false critique, and his self-love would infallibly bias his little judgment in his favor; but a poet, who is indeed a poet, could

not, I think, fail of making-a just critique; whatever should be deducted on the score of self-love might be replaced on account of his intimate acquaintance with the subject; in short, we have more instances of false criticism than of just where one's own writings are the test, simply because we have more bad poets than good. There are, of course, many objections to what I say: Milton is a great example of the contrary; but his opinion with respect to the 'Paradise Regained' is by no means fairly ascertained. By what trivial circumstances men are often led to assert what they do not really believe! Perhaps an inadvertent word has descended to posterity. But, in fact, the 'Paradise Regained' is little, if at all, inferior to the 'Paradise Lost,' and is only supposed so to be because men do not like epics, whatever they may say to the contrary, and, reading those of Milton in their natural order, are too much wearied with the first to derive any pleasure from the second.
"I dare say Milton preferred 'Comus' to either-. if so-justly.
"As I am speaking of poetry, it will not be amiss to touch slightly upon the most singular heresy in its modern history-the heresy of what is called, very foolishly, the Lake School. Some years ago I might have been induced, by an occasion like the present, to attempt a formal refutation of their doctrine; at present it would be a work of supererogation. The wise must bow to the wisdom of such men as Coleridge and Southey, but, being wise, have laughed at poetical theories so prosaically exemplifled.
"Aristotle, with singular assurance, has declared poetry the most philosophical of all writings*-but it required a Wordsworth to pronounce it the most metaphysical. He seems to think that the end of poetry is, or should be, instruction; yet it is a truism that the end of our existence is happiness; if so, the end of every separate part of our existence, everything connected with our existence, should be still happiness. Therefore the end of instruction should be happiness; and

happiness is another name for pleasure;-therefore the end of instruction should be pleasure: yet we see the above-mentioned opinion implies precisely the reverse.

"To proceed: ceteris paribus, he who pleases is of more importance to his fellow-men than he who instructs, since utility is happiness, and pleasure is the end already obtained which instruction is merely the means of obtaining.

"I see no reason, then, why our metaphysical poets should plume themselves so much on the utility of their works, unless indeed they refer to instruction with eternity in view; in which case, sincere respect for their piety would not allow me to express my contempt for their judgment; contempt which it would be difficult to conceal, since their writings are professedly to be understood by the few, and it is the many who stand in need of salvation. In such case I should no doubt be tempted to think of the devil in 'Melmoth.' who labors indefatigably, through three octavo volumes, to accomplish the destruction of one or two souls, while any common devil would have demolished one or two thousand.

"Against the subtleties which would make poetry a study-not a passion-it
becomes the metaphysician to reason-but the poet to protest. Yet Wordsworth and Coleridge are men in years; the one imbued in
contemplation from his childhood; the other a giant in intellect and
learning. The diffidence, then, with which I venture to dispute their
authority would be overwhelming did I not feel, from the bottom of my
heart, that learning has little to do with the imagination-intellect
with the passions-or age with poetry.

"'Trifles, like straws, upon the surface flow;
He who would search for pearls must dive below,'
are lines which have done much mischief. As regards the greater truths, men oftener err by seeking them at the bottom than at the top; Truth lies in the huge abysses where wisdom is sought-not in the palpable palaces where she is found. The ancients were not always right in hiding—the goddess in a well; witness the light which Bacon has thrown upon philosophy; witness the principles of our divine faith—that moral mechanism by which the simplicity of a child may overbalance the wisdom of a man.
"We see an instance of Coleridge's liability to err, in his 'Biographia Literaria'—professedly his literary life and opinions, but, in fact, a treatise de omni scibili et quibusdam aliis. He goes wrong by reason of his very profundity, and of his error we have a natural type in the contemplation of a star. He who regards it directly and intensely sees, it is true, the star, but it is the star without a ray-while he who surveys it less inquisitively is conscious of all for which the star is useful to us below-its brilliancy and its beauty.
"As to Wordsworth, I have no faith in him. That he had in youth the feelings of a poet I believe-for there are glimpses of extreme delicacy in his writings-(and delicacy is the poet's own kingdom-his El Dorado)-but they have the appearance of a better day recollected; and glimpses, at best, are little evidence of present poetic fire; we know that a few straggling flowers spring up daily in the crevices of the glacier.
"He was to blame in wearing away his youth in contemplation with the end of poetizing in his manhood. With the increase of his judgment the light which should make it apparent has faded away. His judgment consequently is too correct. This may not be understood-but the old Goths of Germany would have understood it, who used to debate matters of importance to their State twice, once when drunk,

and once when sober-sober that they might not be deficient in formality—drunk lest they should be destitute of vigor.

"The long wordy discussions by which he tries to reason us into admiration of his poetry, speak very little in his favor: they are full of such assertions as this (I have opened one of his volumes at random)—'Of genius the only proof is the act of doing well what is worthy to be done, and what was never done before;'—indeed? then it follows that in doing what is unworthy to be done, or what has been done before, no genius can be evinced; yet the picking of pockets is an unworthy act, pockets have been picked time immemorial, and Barrington, the pickpocket, in point of genius, would have thought hard of a comparison with William Wordsworth, the poet.

"Again, in estimating the merit of certain poems, whether they be Ossian's or Macpherson's can surely be of little consequence, yet, in order to prove their worthlessness, Mr. W. has expended many pages in the controversy. Tantaene animis? Can great minds descend to such absurdity? But worse still: that he may bear down every argument in favor of these poems, he triumphantly drags forward a passage, in his abomination with which he expects the reader to sympathize. It is the beginning of the epic poem 'Temora.' 'The blue waves of Ullin roll in light; the green hills are covered with day; trees shake their dusty heads in the breeze.' And this this gorgeous, yet simple imagery, where all is alive and panting with immortality-this, William Wordsworth, the author of 'Peter Bell,' has selected for his contempt. We shall see what better he, in his own person, has to offer. Imprimis:

"'And now she's at the pony's tail,
And now she's at the pony's head,
On that side now, and now on this;
And, almost stifled with her bliss,
A few sad tears does Betty shed....
She pats the pony, where or when

>   She knows not.... happy Betty Foy!
>   Oh, Johnny, never mind the doctor!'

Secondly:

>   "'The dew was falling fast, the-stars began to blink;
>   I heard a voice: it said-"Drink, pretty creature, drink!"
>   And, looking o'er the hedge, be-fore me I espied
>   A snow-white mountain lamb, with a-maiden at its side.
>   No other sheep was near,—the lamb was all alone,
>   And by a slender cord was-tether'd to a stone.'

"Now, we have no doubt this is all true: we will believe it, indeed we will, Mr. W. Is it sympathy for the sheep you wish to excite? I love a sheep from the bottom of my heart.

"But there are occasions, dear B-, there are occasions when even Wordsworth is reasonable. Even Stamboul, it is said, shall have an end, and the most unlucky blunders must come to a conclusion. Here is an extract from his preface:-

"'Those who have been accustomed to the phraseology of modem writers, if they persist in reading this book to a conclusion (impossible!) will, no doubt, have to struggle with feelings of awkwardness; (ha! ha! ha!) they will look round for poetry (ha! ha! ha! ha!), and will be induced to inquire by what species of courtesy these attempts have been permitted to assume that title.' Ha! ha! ha! ha! ha!

"Yet, let not Mr. W. despair; he has given immortality to a wagon, and the bee Sophocles has transmitted to eternity a sore toe, and dignified a tragedy with a chorus of turkeys.

"Of Coleridge, I can not speak but with reverence. His towering intellect! his gigantic power! To use an author quoted by himself, 'Tai trouvé souvent que la plupart des sectes ont raison dans une bonne partie de ce qu'elles avancent, mais non pas en ce qu'elles nient,' and to employ his own language, he has imprisoned his own conceptions by the barrier he has erected against those of others. It is lamentable to think that such a mind should be buried in metaphysics, and, like the

Nyctanthes, waste its perfume upon the night alone. In reading that man's poetry, I tremble like one who stands upon a volcano, conscious from the very darkness bursting from the crater, of the fire and the light that are weltering below.
"What is poetry?—Poetry! that Proteus-like idea, with as many appellations as the nine-titled Corcyra! 'Give me,' I demanded of a scholar some time ago, 'give me a definition of poetry.' 'Trésvolontiers;' and he proceeded to his library, brought me a Dr. Johnson, and overwhelmed me with a definition. Shade of the immortal Shakespeare! I imagine to myself the scowl of your spiritual eye upon the profanity of that scurrilous Ursa Major. Think of poetry, dear B-, think of poetry, and then think of Dr. Samuel Johnson! Think of all that is airy and fairy-like, and then of all that is hideous and unwieldy; think of his huge bulk, the Elephant! and then-and then think of the 'Tempest'—the 'Midsummer-Night's Dream'—Prospero Oberon—and Titania!
"A poem, in my opinion, is opposed to a work of science by having, for its immediate object, pleasure, not truth; to romance, by having, for its object, an indefinite instead of a definite pleasure, being a poem only so far as this object is attained; romance presenting perceptible images with definite, poetry with indefinite sensations, to which end music is an essential, since the comprehension of sweet sound is our most indefinite conception. Music, when combined with a pleasurable idea, is poetry; music, without the idea, is simply music; the idea, without the music, is prose, from its very definitiveness.
"What was meant by the invective against him who had no music in his soul?
"To sum up this long rigmarole, I have, dear B—, what you, no doubt, perceive, for the metaphysical poets as poets, the most sovereign contempt. That they have followers proves nothing-

"'No Indian prince has to his palace
More followers than a thief to the gallows.

 Al Aaraaf

PART I.

    O! Nothing earthly save the ray
    (Thrown back from flowers) of Beauty's eye,
    As in those gardens where the day
    Springs from the gems of Circassy—
    O! nothing earthly save the thrill
    Of melody in woodland rill—
    Or (music of the passion-hearted)
    Joy's voice so peacefully departed
    That like the murmur in the shell,
    Its echo dwelleth and will dwell—
    Oh, nothing of the dross of ours—
    Yet all the beauty—all the flowers
    That list our Love, and deck our bowers—
    Adorn yon world afar, afar—
    The wandering star.

      'Twas a sweet time for Nesace—for there
    Her world lay lolling on the golden air,
    Near four bright suns—a temporary rest—
    An oasis in desert of the blest.

* A star was discovered by Tycho Brahe which appeared suddenly in the heavens—attained, in a few days, a brilliancy surpassing that of Jupiter—then as suddenly disappeared, and has never been seen since.

    Away—away—'mid seas of rays that roll
    Empyrean splendor o'er th' unchained soul—
    The soul that scarce (the billows are so dense)
    Can struggle to its destin'd eminence—
    To distant spheres, from time to time, she rode,
    And late to ours, the favour'd one of God—

But, now, the ruler of an anchor'd realm,
She throws aside the sceptre—leaves the helm,
And, amid incense and high spiritual hymns,
Laves in quadruple light her angel limbs.

    Now happiest, loveliest in yon lovely Earth,
Whence sprang the "Idea of Beauty" into birth,
(Falling in wreaths thro' many a startled star,
Like woman's hair 'mid pearls, until, afar,
It lit on hills Achaian, and there dwelt)
She look'd into Infinity—and knelt.
Rich clouds, for canopies, about her curled—
Fit emblems of the model of her world—
Seen but in beauty—not impeding sight
Of other beauty glittering thro' the light—
A wreath that twined each starry form around,
And all the opal'd air in color bound.
All hurriedly she knelt upon a bed
Of flowers: of lilies such as rear'd the head
*On the fair Capo Deucato, and sprang
So eagerly around about to hang
Upon the flying footsteps of—deep pride—
**Of her who lov'd a mortal—and so died.
The Sephalica, budding with young bees,
Uprear'd its purple stem around her knees:
* On Santa Maura—olim Deucadia.
**And gemmy flower, of Trebizond misnam'd—
Inmate of highest stars, where erst it sham'd
All other loveliness: its honied dew
(The fabled nectar that the heathen knew)
Deliriously sweet, was dropp'd from Heaven,
And fell on gardens of the unforgiven
In Trebizond—and on a sunny flower
So like its own above that, to this hour,
It still remaineth, torturing the bee

With madness, and unwonted reverie:
In Heaven, and all its environs, the leaf
And blossom of the fairy plant, in grief
Disconsolate linger—grief that hangs her head,
Repenting follies that full long have fled,
Heaving her white breast to the balmy air,
Like guilty beauty, chasten'd, and more fair:
Nyctanthes too, as sacred as the light
She fears to perfume, perfuming the night:
**And Clytia pondering between many a sun,
While pettish tears adown her petals run:
***And that aspiring flower that sprang on Earth—
And died, ere scarce exalted into birth,
Bursting its odorous heart in spirit to wing
Its way to Heaven, from garden of a king:

 * This flower is much noticed by Lewenhoeck and Tournefort.

 The bee, feeding upon its blossom, becomes intoxicated.
 ** Clytia—The Chrysanthemum Peruvianum, or, to employ a
 better-known term, the turnsol—which continually turns towards the sun, covers itself, like Peru, the country from which it comes, with dewy clouds which cool and refresh its
 flowers during the most violent heat of the day.—B. de St. Pierre.
 *** There is cultivated in the king's garden at Paris, a species of serpentine aloes without prickles, whose large and beautiful flower exhales a strong odour of the vanilla, during the time of its expansion, which is very short. It does not blow till towards the month of July—you then perceive it gradually open its petals—expand them—fade and die.—St. Pierre.
 *And Valisnerian lotus thither flown

From struggling with the waters of the Rhone:
**And thy most lovely purple perfume, Zante!
Isola d'oro!—Fior di Levante!
***And the Nelumbo bud that floats for ever
With Indian Cupid down the holy river—
Fair flowers, and fairy! to whose care is given
****To bear the Goddess' song, in odors, up to Heaven:
   "Spirit! that dwellest where,
     In the deep sky,
    The terrible and fair,
     In beauty vie!
   Beyond the line of blue—
     The boundary of the star
   Which turneth at the view
     Of thy barrier and thy bar—
   Of the barrier overgone
     By the comets who were cast
   From their pride, and from their throne
     To be drudges till the last—
   To be carriers of fire
     (The red fire of their heart)
   With speed that may not tire
     And with pain that shall not part—

* There is found, in the Rhone, a beautiful lily of the Valisnerian kind. Its stem will stretch to the length of three or four feet—thus preserving its head above water in the swellings of the river.

** The Hyacinth.

*** It is a fiction of the Indians, that Cupid was first seen floating in one of these down the river Ganges—and that he still loves the cradle of his childhood.

**** And golden vials full of odors which are the prayers of the saints.

  —Rev. St. John.

Who livest—*that we know*—
    In Eternity—we feel—
But the shadow of whose brow
    What spirit shall reveal?
Tho' the beings whom thy Nesace,
    Thy messenger hath known
Have dream'd for thy Infinity
    *A model of their own—
Thy will is done, Oh, God!
    The star hath ridden high
Thro' many a tempest, but she rode
    Beneath thy burning eye;
And here, in thought, to thee—
    In thought that can alone
Ascend thy empire and so be
    A partner of thy throne—

* The Humanitarians held that God was to be understood as having a really human form.—*Vide Clarke's Sermons*, vol. 1, page 26, fol. edit.

The drift of Milton's argument, leads him to employ language which would appear, at first sight, to verge upon their doctrine; but it will be seen immediately, that he guards himself against the charge of having adopted one of the most ignorant errors of the dark ages of the church.—*Dr. Sumner's Notes on Milton's Christian Doctrine.*

This opinion, in spite of many testimonies to the contrary, could never have been very general. Andeus, a Syrian of Mesopotamia, was condemned for the opinion, as heretical. He lived in the beginning of the fourth century. His disciples were called Anthropmorphites.—*Vide Du Pin.*

Among Milton's poems are these lines:—
>Dicite sacrorum præsides nemorum Deæ, &c.
>Quis ille primus cujus ex imagine
>Natura solers finxit humanum genus?
>Eternus, incorruptus, æquævus polo,
>Unusque et universus exemplar Dei.—And

afterwards,
>Non cui profundum Cæcitas lumen dedit
>Dircæus augur vidit hunc alto sinu, &c.

*By winged Fantasy,
   My embassy is given,
Till secrecy shall knowledge be
   In the environs of Heaven."
She ceas'd—and buried then her burning cheek
Abash'd, amid the lilies there, to seek
A shelter from the fervour of His eye;
For the stars trembled at the Deity.
She stirr'd not—breath'd not—for a voice was there
How solemnly pervading the calm air!
A sound of silence on the startled ear
Which dreamy poets name "the music of the sphere."
Ours is a world of words: Quiet we call
"Silence"—which is the merest word of all.
All Nature speaks, and ev'n ideal things
Flap shadowy sounds from visionary wings—
But ah! not so when, thus, in realms on high
The eternal voice of God is passing by,
And the red winds are withering in the sky!
**"What tho' in worlds which sightless cycles run,
Link'd to a little system, and one sun—
Where all my love is folly and the crowd
Still think my terrors but the thunder cloud,
The storm, the earthquake, and the ocean-wrath—
(Ah! will they cross me in my angrier path?)

What tho' in worlds which own a single sun
The sands of Time grow dimmer as they run,
* Seltsamen Tochter Jovis
Seinem Schosskinde
Der Phantasie.—*Göethe*.
** Sightless—too small to be seen—*Legge*.
Yet thine is my resplendency, so given
To bear my secrets thro' the upper Heaven.
Leave tenantless thy crystal home, and fly,
With all thy train, athwart the moony sky—
*Apart—like fire-flies in Sicilian night,
And wing to other worlds another light!
Divulge the secrets of thy embassy
To the proud orbs that twinkle—and so be
To ev'ry heart a barrier and a ban
Lest the stars totter in the guilt of man!"
Up rose the maiden in the yellow night,
The single-mooned eve!—on Earth we plight
Our faith to one love—and one moon adore—
The birth-place of young Beauty had no more.
As sprang that yellow star from downy hours
Up rose the maiden from her shrine of flowers,
And bent o'er sheeny mountain and dim plain
**Her way—but left not yet her Therasæan reign.
* I have often noticed a peculiar movement of the fire-flies; —they will collect in a body and fly off, from a common centre, into innumerable radii.
** Therasæa, or Therasea, the island mentioned by Seneca, which, in a moment, arose from the sea to the eyes of astonished mariners.

Part II.
HIGH on a mountain of enamell'd head—
Such as the drowsy shepherd on his bed

Of giant pasturage lying at his ease,
Raising his heavy eyelid, starts and sees
With many a mutter'd "hope to be forgiven"
What time the moon is quadrated in Heaven—
Of rosy head, that towering far away
Into the sunlit ether, caught the ray
Of sunken suns at eve—at noon of night,
While the moon danc'd with the fair stranger light—
Uprear'd upon such height arose a pile
Of gorgeous columns on th' unburthen'd air,
Flashing from Parian marble that twin smile
Far down upon the wave that sparkled there,
And nursled the young mountain in its lair.
*Of molten stars their pavement, such as fall
Thro' the ebon air, besilvering the pall
Of their own dissolution, while they die—
Adorning then the dwellings of the sky.
A dome, by linked light from Heaven let down,
Sat gently on these columns as a crown—
A window of one circular diamond, there,
Look'd out above into the purple air,

* Some star which, from the ruin'd roof Of shak'd Olympus, by mischance, did fall.—*Milton.*

And rays from God shot down that meteor chain
And hallow'd all the beauty twice again,
Save when, between th' Empyrean and that ring,
Some eager spirit flapp'd his dusky wing.
But on the pillars Seraph eyes have seen
The dimness of this world: that greyish green
That Nature loves the best for Beauty's grave
Lurk'd in each cornice, round each architrave—
And every sculptur'd cherub thereabout
That from his marble dwelling peeréd out
Seem'd earthly in the shadow of his niche—

87

Achaian statues in a world so rich?
*Friezes from Tadmor and Persepolis—
From Balbec, and the stilly, clear abyss
**Of beautiful Gomorrah! O, the wave
Is now upon thee—but too late to save!
Sound loves to revel in a summer night:
Witness the murmur of the grey twilight

* Voltaire, in speaking of Persepolis, says, "Je connois
bien l'admiration qu'inspirent ces ruines—mais un palais
erigé au pied d'une chaine des rochers sterils—peut il
être un chef d'oevure des arts!" [*Voila les arguments de M.
Voltaire.*]

** "Oh! the wave"—Ula Degusi is the Turkish appellation;
but, on its own shores, it is called Bahar Loth, or
Almotanah. There were undoubtedly more than two cities
engluphed in the "dead sea." In the valley of Siddim were
five—Adrah, Zeboin, Zoar, Sodom and Gomorrah. Stephen
of
Byzantium mentions eight, and Strabo thirteeen, (engulphed)
—but the last is out of all reason.

It is said, (Tacitus, Strabo, Josephus, Daniel of St. Saba, Nau,
Maundrell, Troilo, D'Arvieux) that after an excessive drought,
the
vestiges of columns, walls, &c. are seen above the surface. At
any
season, such remains may be discovered by looking down into
the
transparent lake, and at such distances as would argue the
existence of
many settlements in the space now usurped by the
'Asphaltites.'

*That stole upon the ear, in Eyraco,
Of many a wild star-gazer long ago—

That stealeth ever on the ear of him
Who, musing, gazeth on the distance dim.
And sees the darkness coming as a cloud—
***Is not its form—its voice—most palpable and loud?
   But what is this?—it cometh—and it brings
A music with it—'tis the rush of wings—
A pause—and then a sweeping, falling strain
And Nesace is in her halls again.
From the wild energy of wanton haste
   Her cheeks were flushing, and her lips apart;
And zone that clung around her gentle waist
   Had burst beneath the heaving of her heart.
Within the centre of that hall to breathe
She paus'd and panted, Zanthe! all beneath,
The fairy light that kiss'd her golden hair
And long'd to rest, yet could but sparkle there!
   ***Young flowers were whispering in melody
To happy flowers that night—and tree to tree;
Fountains were gushing music as they fell
In many a star-lit grove, or moon-lit dell;
Yet silence came upon material things—
Fair flowers, bright waterfalls and angel wings—
And sound alone that from the spirit sprang
Bore burthen to the charm the maiden sang:

* Eyraco—Chaldea.
** I have often thought I could distinctly hear the sound of the darkness as it stole over the horizon.
*** Fairies use flowers for their charactery.—*Merry Wives of Windsor.* [William Shakespeare]

   "'Neath blue-bell or streamer—
     Or tufted wild spray
   That keeps, from the dreamer,
     *The moonbeam away—
   Bright beings! that ponder,

With half closing eyes,
　On the stars which your wonder
　　　　Hath drawn from the skies,
　Till they glance thro' the shade, and
　　　　Come down to your brow
　Like—eyes of the maiden
　　　　Who calls on you now—
　Arise! from your dreaming
　　　　In violet bowers,
　To duty beseeming
　　　　These star-litten hours—
　And shake from your tresses
　　　　Encumber'd with dew
　The breath of those kisses
　　　　That cumber them too—
　(O! how, without you, Love!
　　　　Could angels be blest?)
　Those kisses of true love
　　　　That lull'd ye to rest!
　Up!—shake from your wing
　　　　Each hindering thing:
　The dew of the night—
　　　　It would weigh down your flight;
　And true love caresses—
　　　　O! leave them apart!

* In Scripture is this passage—"The sun shall not harm thee by day, nor the moon by night." It is perhaps not generally known that the moon, in Egypt, has the effect of producing blindness to those who sleep with the face exposed
　　to its rays, to which circumstance the passage evidently alludes.

　　　They are light on the tresses,
　　　　But lead on the heart.

Ligeia! Ligeia!
  My beautiful one!
Whose harshest idea
  Will to melody run,
O! is it thy will
  On the breezes to toss?
Or, capriciously still,
  *Like the lone Albatross,
Incumbent on night
  (As she on the air)
To keep watch with delight
  On the harmony there?
Ligeia! whatever
  Thy image may be,
No magic shall sever
  Thy music from thee.
Thou hast bound many eyes
  In a dreamy sleep—
But the strains still arise
  Which *thy* vigilance keep—
The sound of the rain
  Which leaps down to the flower,
And dances again
  In the rhythm of the shower—
**The murmur that springs
  From the growing of grass

* The Albatross is said to sleep on the wing.
** I met with this idea in an old English tale, which I am now unable to obtain and quote from memory:—"The verie essence and, as it were, springe-heade, and origine of all musiche is the verie pleasaunte sounde which the trees of the forest do make when they growe."

  Are the music of things—
    But are modell'd, alas!—

Away, then my dearest,
   O! hie thee away
To springs that lie clearest
   Beneath the moon-ray—
To lone lake that smiles,
   In its dream of deep rest,
At the many star-isles
   That enjewel its breast—
Where wild flowers, creeping,
   Have mingled their shade,
On its margin is sleeping
   Full many a maid—
Some have left the cool glade, and
   * Have slept with the bee—
Arouse them my maiden,
   On moorland and lea—
Go! breathe on their slumber,
   All softly in ear,
The musical number
   They slumber'd to hear—
For what can awaken
   An angel so soon

* The wild bee will not sleep in the shade if there be moonlight. The rhyme in this verse, as in one about sixty lines before, has an appearance of affectation. It is, however, imitated from Sir W. Scott, or rather from Claud Halcro—in whose mouth I admired its effect:

   O! were there an island,
      Tho' ever so wild
    Where woman might smile, and
      No man be beguil'd, &c.

Whose sleep hath been taken
   Beneath the cold moon,
As the spell which no slumber

>   Of witchery may test,
>   The rythmical number
>   Which lull'd him to rest?"
> Spirits in wing, and angels to the view,
> A thousand seraphs burst th' Empyrean thro',
> Young dreams still hovering on their drowsy flight—
> Seraphs in all but "Knowledge," the keen light
> That fell, refracted, thro' thy bounds, afar
> O Death! from eye of God upon that star:
> Sweet was that error—sweeter still that death—
> Sweet was that error—ev'n with us the breath
> Of science dims the mirror of our joy—
> To them 'twere the Simoom, and would destroy—
> For what (to them) availeth it to know
> That Truth is Falsehood—or that Bliss is Woe?
> Sweet was their death—with them to die was rife
> With the last ecstacy of satiate life—
> Beyond that death no immortality—
> But sleep that pondereth and is not "to be"—
> And there—oh! may my weary spirit dwell—
>   *Apart from Heaven's Eternity—and yet how far from Hell!

* With the Arabians there is a medium between Heaven and
   Hell, where men suffer no punishment, but yet do not attain
   that tranquil and even happiness which they suppose to be
   characteristic of heavenly enjoyment.

>   Un no rompido sueno—
>   Un dia puro—allegre—libre
>   Quiera—
>   Libre de amor—de zelo—
>   De odio—de esperanza—de rezelo.—-*Luis Ponce de Leon.*
> Sorrow is not excluded from "Al Aaraaf," but it is that

sorrow which the living love to cherish for the dead, and which, in some minds, resembles the delirium of opium. The passionate excitement of Love and the buoyancy of spirit attendant upon intoxication are its less holy pleasures—the price of which, to those souls who make choice of "Al Aaraaf" as their residence after life, is final death and annihilation.

    What guilty spirit, in what shrubbery dim,
Heard not the stirring summons of that hymn?
But two: they fell: for Heaven no grace imparts
To those who hear not for their beating hearts.
A maiden-angel and her seraph-lover—
O! where (and ye may seek the wide skies over)
Was Love, the blind, near sober Duty known?
*Unguided Love hath fallen—'mid "tears of perfect moan."
He was a goodly spirit—he who fell:
A wanderer by moss-y-mantled well—
A gazer on the lights that shine above—
A dreamer in the moonbeam by his love:
What wonder? For each star is eye-like there,
And looks so sweetly down on Beauty's hair—
And they, and ev'ry mossy spring were holy
To his love-haunted heart and melancholy.
The night had found (to him a night of wo)
Upon a mountain crag, young Angelo—
Beetling it bends athwart the solemn sky,
And scowls on starry worlds that down beneath it lie.
Here sate he with his love—his dark eye bent
With eagle gaze along the firmament:
Now turn'd it upon her—but ever then
It trembled to the orb of EARTH again.
"Iante, dearest, see! how dim that ray!
How lovely 'tis to look so far away!

* There be tears of perfect moan

Wept for thee in Helicon.—*Milton*.
She seem'd not thus upon that autumn eve
I left her gorgeous halls—nor mourn'd to leave.
That eve—that eve—I should remember well—
The sun-ray dropp'd, in Lemnos, with a spell
On th'Arabesque carving of a gilded hall
Wherein I sate, and on the draperied wall—
And on my eye-lids—O the heavy light!
How drowsily it weigh'd them into night!
On flowers, before, and mist, and love they ran
With Persian Saadi in his Gulistan:
But O that light!—I slumber'd—Death, the while,
Stole o'er my senses in that lovely isle
So softly that no single silken hair
Awoke that slept—or knew that it was there.
The last spot of Earth's orb I trod upon
*Was a proud temple call'd the Parthenon—
More beauty clung around her column'd wall
**Than ev'n thy glowing bosom beats withal,
And when old Time my wing did disenthral
Thence sprang I—as the eagle from his tower,
And years I left behind me in an hour.
What time upon her airy bounds I hung
One half the garden of her globe was flung
Unrolling as a chart unto my view—
Tenantless cities of the desert too!
Ianthe, beauty crowded on me then,
And half I wish'd to be again of men."
"My Angelo! and why of them to be?
A brighter dwelling-place is here for thee—

* It was entire in 1687—the most elevated spot in Athens.
** Shadowing more beauty in their airy brows
Than have the white breasts of the Queen of Love.—
Marlowe.

And greener fields than in yon world above,
And women's loveliness—and passionate love."
"But, list, Ianthe! when the air so soft
*Fail'd, as my pennon'd spirit leapt aloft,
Perhaps my brain grew dizzy—but the world
I left so late was into chaos hurl'd—
Sprang from her station, on the winds apart,
And roll'd, a flame, the fiery Heaven athwart.
Methought, my sweet one, then I ceased to soar
And fell—not swiftly as I rose before,
But with a downward, tremulous motion thro'
Light, brazen rays, this golden star unto!
Nor long the measure of my falling hours,
For nearest of all stars was thine to ours—
Dread star! that came, amid a night of mirth,
A red Dædalion on the timid Earth.
"We came—and to thy Earth—but not to us
Be given our lady's bidding to discuss:
We came, my love; around, above, below,
Gay fire-fly of the night we come and go,
Nor ask a reason save the angel-nod
She grants to us, as granted by her God—
But, Angelo, than thine grey Time unfurl'd
Never his fairy wing o'er fairier world!
Dim was its little disk, and angel eyes
Alone could see the phantom in the skies,
When first Al Aaraaf knew her course to be
Headlong thitherward o'er the starry sea—
But when its glory swell'd upon the sky,
As glowing Beauty's bust beneath man's eye,

* Pennon—for pinion.—*Milton.*

We paus'd before the heritage of men,
And thy star trembled—as doth Beauty then!"
Thus, in discourse, the lovers whiled away

The night that waned and waned and brought no day.

They fell: for Heaven to them no hope imparts
Who hear not for the beating of their hearts.

Tamerlane

KIND solace in a dying hour!
Such, father, is not (now) my theme— I will not madly deem that power
Of Earth may shrive me of the sin Unearthly pride hath revell'd in—
I have no time to dote or dream: You call it hope—that fire of fire!
It is but agony of desire:
If I can hope—Oh God! I can—
Its fount is holier—more divine— I would not call thee fool, old man,
But such is not a gift of thine.
Know thou the secret of a spirit
Bow'd from its wild pride into shame.
O! yearning heart! I did inherit
Thy withering portion with the fame, The searing glory which hath shone Amid the jewels of my throne,
Halo of Hell! and with a pain
Not Hell shall make me fear again— O! craving heart, for the lost flowers And sunshine of my summer hours! Th' undying voice of that dead time, With its interminable chime,
Rings, in the spirit of a spell, Upon thy emptiness—a knell.

I have not always been as now: The fever'd diadem on my brow
I claim'd and won usurpingly—
Hath not the same fierce heirdom given Rome to the Caesar— this to me?
The heritage of a kingly mind, And a proud spirit which hath striven

Triumphantly with human kind.

On mountain soil I first drew life:
The mists of the Taglay have shed Nightly their dews upon my head,
And, I believe, the winged strife And tumult of the headlong air Have nestled in my very hair.

So late from Heaven—that dew—it fell (Mid dreams of an unholy night)
Upon me—with the touch of Hell, While the red flashing of the light
From clouds that hung, like banners, o'er, Appeared to my half-closing eye
The pageantry of monarchy,
And the deep trumpet-thunder's roar Came hurriedly upon me, telling
Of human battle, where my voice,
My own voice, silly child!—was swelling (O! how my spirit would rejoice,
And leap within me at the cry) The battle-cry of Victory!

The rain came down upon my head Unshelter'd—and the heavy wind Was giantlike—so thou, my mind!—
It was but man, I thought, who shed Laurels upon me: and the rush—
The torrent of the chilly air Gurgled within my ear the crush
Of empires—with the captive's prayer— The hum of suiters—and the tone
Of flattery 'round a sovereign's throne.

My passions, from that hapless hour, Usurp'd a tyranny which men

Have deem'd, since I have reach'd to power; My innate nature—be it so:
But, father, there liv'd one who, then, Then—in my boyhood—when their fire
Burn'd with a still intenser glow, (For passion must, with youth, expire)
E'en then who knew this iron heart In woman's weakness had a part.

I have no words—alas!—to tell The loveliness of loving well!
Nor would I now attempt to trace The more than beauty of a face Whose lineaments, upon my mind, Are—shadows on th' unstable wind: Thus I remember having dwelt Some page of early lore upon,
With loitering eye, till I have felt
The letters—with their meaning—melt To fantasies—with none.

O, she was worthy of all love! Love—as in infancy was mine—
'Twas such as angel minds above Might envy; her young heart the shrine On which my ev'ry hope and thought
Were incense—then a goodly gift,
For they were childish—and upright— Pure—as her young example taught:
Why did I leave it, and, adrift, Trust to the fire within, for light?

We grew in age—and love—together, Roaming the forest, and the wild;
My breast her shield in wintry weather— And, when the friendly sunshine smil'd,
And she would mark the opening skies,
I saw no Heaven—but in her eyes.

Young Love's first lesson is—the heart:

For 'mid that sunshine, and those smiles, When, from our little cares apart,
And laughing at her girlish wiles, I'd throw me on her throbbing breast,
And pour my spirit out in tears— There was no need to speak the rest—
No need to quiet any fears
Of her—who ask'd no reason why, But turn'd on me her quiet eye!

Yet more than worthy of the love

My spirit struggled with, and strove, When, on the mountain peak, alone, Ambition lent it a new tone—
I had no being—but in thee:
The world, and all it did contain In the earth—the air—the sea—
Its joy—its little lot of pain
That was new pleasure—the ideal, Dim, vanities of dreams by night—
And dimmer nothings which were real— (Shadows—and a more shadowy light!)
Parted upon their misty wings, And, so, c onfusedly, became
Thine image, and—a name—a name!
Two separate—yet most intimate things.

I was ambitious—have you known
The passion, father? You have not: A cottager, I mark'd a throne
Of half the world as all my own,
And murmur'd at such lowly lot— But, just like any other dream,
Upon the vapour of the dew My own had past, did not the beam

Of beauty which did while it thro' The minute—the hour—the day—oppress My mind with double loveliness.

We walk'd together on the crown
Of a high mountain which look'd down Afar from its proud natural towers
Of rock and forest, on the hills— The dwindled hills! begirt with bowers
And shouting with a thousand rills.

I spoke to her of power and pride, But mystically—in such guise
That she might deem it nought beside The moment's converse; in her eyes
I read, perhaps too carelessly—
A mingled feeling with my own— The flush on her bright cheek, to me
Seem'd to become a queenly throne

Too well that I should let it be Light in the wilderness alone.

I wrapp'd myself in grandeur then, And donn'd a visionary crown—
Yet it was not that Fantasy
Had thrown her mantle over me— But that, among the rabble—men,
Lion ambition is chain'd down— And crouches to a keeper's hand— Not so in deserts where the grand The wild—the terrible conspire
With their own breath to fan his fire.

Look 'round thee now on Samarcand!— Is not she queen of Earth? her pride
Above all cities? in her hand Their destinies? in all beside

Of glory which the world hath known Stands she not nobly and alone?
Falling—her veriest stepping-stone Shall form the pedestal of a throne— And who her sovereign? Timour—he
Whom the astonished people saw Striding o'er empires haughtily
A diadem'd outlaw—

O! human love! thou spirit given, On Earth, of all we hope in Heaven! Which fall'st into the soul like rain Upon the Siroc wither'd plain,
And failing in thy power to bless But leav'st the heart a wilderness! Idea! which bindest life around With music of so strange a sound And beauty of so wild a birth— Farewell! for I have won the Earth!

When Hope, the eagle that tower'd, could see No cliff beyond him in the sky,
His pinions were bent droopingly—
And homeward turn'd his soften'd eye. 'Twas sunset: when the sun will part

There comes a sullenness of heart To him who still would look upon The glory of the summer sun.
That soul will hate the ev'ning mist, So often lovely, and will list
To the sound of the coming darkness (known To those whose spirits hearken) as one Who, in a dream of night, would fly But cannot from a danger nigh.

What tho' the moon—the white moon Shed all the splendour of her noon, Her smile is chilly—and her beam,
In that time of dreariness, will seem (So like you gather in your breath) A portrait taken after death.

And boyhood is a summer sun Whose waning is the dreariest one— For all we live to know is known,
And all we seek to keep hath flown— Let life, then, as the day-flower, fall With the noon-day beauty—which is all.

I reach'd my home—my home no more— For all had flown who made it so—
I pass'd from out its mossy door,
And, tho' my tread was soft and low, A voice came from the threshold stone Of one whom I had earlier known—
O! I defy thee, Hell, to show On beds of fire that burn below, A humbler heart—a deeper wo—

Father, I firmly do believe—
I know—for Death, who comes for me From regions of the blest afar,
Where there is nothing to deceive, Hath left his iron gate ajar,
And rays of truth you cannot see Are flashing thro' Eternity—
I do believe that Eblis hath
A snare in ev'ry human path— Else how, when in the holy grove

I wandered of the idol, Love,
Who daily scents his snowy wings With incense of burnt offerings From the most unpolluted things,
Whose pleasant bowers are yet so riven Above with trelliced rays from Heaven No mote may shun—no tiniest fly
The light'ning of his eagle eye— How was it that Ambition crept,
Unseen, amid the revels there,
Till growing bold, he laughed and leapt In the tangles of Love's very hair?
1829.

To Helen

HELEN, thy beauty is to me
Like those Nicean barks of yore, That gently, o'er a perfumed sea,
The weary way-worn wanderer bore To his own native shore.

On desperate seas long wont to roam, Thy hyacinth hair, thy classic face,
Thy Naiad airs have brought me home To the glory that was Greece,
And the grandeur that was Rome.

Lo! in yon brilliant window-niche How statue-like I me thee stand,
The agate lamp within thy hand!
Ah, Psyche, from the regions which Are Holy-land!

The Valley Of Unrest

Once it smiled a silent dell Where the people did not dwell;
They had gone unto the wars, Trusting to the mild-eyed stars,
Nightly, from their azure towers,
To keep watch above the flowers, In the midst of which all day
The red sun-light lazily lay. Now each visiter shall confess The sad valley's restlessness. Nothing there is motionless—
Nothing save the airs that brood Over the magic solitude.
Ah, by no wind are stirred those trees That palpitate like the chill seas Around the misty Hebrides!
Ah, by no wind those clouds are driven That rustle through the unquiet Heaven Uneasily, from morn till even,
Over the violets there that lie
In myriad types of the human eye— Over the lilies there that wave
And weep above a nameless grave! They wave:—from out their fragrant tops Eternal dews come down in drops.
They weep:—from off their delicate stems Perennial tears descend in gems.

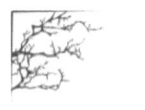

Israfel*

IN Heaven a spirit doth dwell "Whose heart-strings are a lute;"
None sing so wildly well As the angel Israfel,
And the giddy stars (so legends tell) Ceasing their hymns, attend the spell
Of his voice, all mute.

Tottering above
In her highest noon The enamoured moon
Blushes with love,
While, to listen, the red levin (With the rapid Pleiads, even,
Which were seven,)
Pauses in Heaven

And they say (the starry choir And all the listening things)
That Israfeli's fire Is owing to that lyre
By which he sits and sings— The trembling living wire
Of those unusual strings.

* And the angel Israfel, whose heart-strings are a lut, and who has the sweetest voice of all God's creatures.—KORAN.

But the skies that angel trod,
Where deep thoughts are a duty— Where Love's a grown up God—
Where the Houri glances are Imbued with all the beauty
Which we worship in a star.

Therefore, thou art not wrong, Israfeli, who despisest

An unimpassion'd song:

To thee the laurels belong
Best bard, because the wisest!
Merrily live, and long!

The extacies above
With thy burning measures suit— Thy grief, thy joy, thy hate, thy love,
With the fervor of thy lute— Well may the stars be mute!

Yes, Heaven is thine; but this
Is a world of sweets and sours; Our flowers are merely—
flowers,
And the shadow of thy perfect bliss Is the sunshine of ours.

If I could dwell Where Israfel
Hath dwelt, and he where I, He might not sing so wildly well
A mortal melody,
While a bolder note than this might swell From my lyre within the sky.

 To ---- Z Z

1
The bowers whereat, in dreams, I see The wantonest singing birds
Are lips—and all thy melody Of lip-begotten words—
2
Thine eyes, in Heaven of heart enshrin'd Then desolately fall,
O! God! on my funereal mind Like starlight on a pall—
3
Thy heart—thy heart!—I wake and sigh, And sleep to dream till day
Of truth that gold can never buy— Of the trifles that it may.

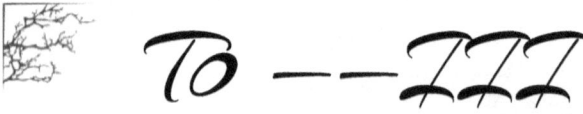 To ——III

I HEED not that my earthly lot Hath-little of Earth in it—
That years of love have been forgot In the hatred of a minute:—
I mourn not that the desolate Are happier, sweet, than I,
But that you sorrow for my fate Who am a passer-by.

To The River——

FAIR river! in thy bright, clear flow Of crystal, wandering water,
Thou art an emblem of the glow
Of beauty—the unhidden heart— The playful maziness of art
In old Alberto's daughter;

But when within thy wave she looks— Which glistens then, and trembles—
Why, then, the prettiest of brooks Her worshipper resembles;
For in my heart, as in thy stream, Her image deeply lies—
His heart which trembles at the beam Of her soul-searching eyes.

Song

I SAW thee on thy bridal day—
When a burning blush came o'er thee, Though happiness around thee lay,
The world all love before thee:

And in thine eye a kindling light (Whatever it might be)
Was all on Earth my aching sight Of Loveliness could see.

That blush, perhaps, was maiden shame— As such it well may pass—
Though its glow hath raised a fiercer flame In the breast of him, alas!

Who saw thee on that bridal day,
When that deep blush would come o'er thee, Though happiness around thee lay,
The world all love before thee.

Spirits Of The Dead

1
Thy soul shall find itself alone
'Mid dark thoughts of the grey tomb-stone— Not one, of all the crowd, to pry
Into thine hour of secrecy:
2
Be silent in that solitude
Which is not loneliness—for then The spirits of the dead who stood
In life before thee are again
In death around thee—and their will Shall then overshadow thee: be still.
3
For the night—tho' clear—shall frown— An d the stars shall look not down, From their high thrones in the Heaven, With light like Hope to mortals given— But their red orbs, without beam,
To thy weariness shall seem As a burning and a fever
Which would cling to thee for ever:
4
Now are thoughts thou shalt not banish— Now are visions ne'er to vanish—
From thy spirit shall they pass
No more—like dew-drop from the grass:
5
The breeze—the breath of God—is still—
And the mist upon the hill Shadowy—shadowy—yet unbroken,
Is a symbol and a token—
How it hangs upon the trees, A mystery of mysteries!—

A Dream

In visions of the dark night
I have dreamed of joy departed— But a waking dreams of life and light
Hath left me broken-hearted.

Ah! what is not a dream by day To him whose eyes are cast
On things around him with a ray
Turned back upon the past?

That holy dream—that holy dream, While all the world were chiding, Hath cheered me as a lovely beam
A lonely spirit guiding.

What though that light, thro' storm and night, So trembled from afar-
What could there be more purely bright In Truths day-star?

Romance

ROMANCE, who loves to nod and sing, With drowsy head and folded wing, Among the green leaves as they shake Far down within some shadowy lake, To me a painted paroquet Hath been—a most familiar bird— Taught me my alphabet to say— To lisp my very earliest word While in the wild wood I did lie,
A child—with a most knowing eye.

Of late, eternal Condor years
So shake the very Heaven on high With tumult as they thunder by,
I have no time for idle cares Through gazing on the unquiet sky. And when an hour with calmer wings Its down upon thy spirit flings—
That little time with lyre and rhyme To while away—forbidden things! My heart would feel to be a crime Unless it trembled with the strings.

1829.

Fairy-Land

DIM vales—and shadowy floods— And cloudy-looking woods,
Whose forms we can't discover For the tears that drip all over
Huge moons there wax and waine— Again—again—again—
Every moment of the night— Forever changing places— And
they put out the star-light

With the breath from their pale faces. About twelve by the moon-dial
One, more filmy than the rest (A kind which, upon trial,
They have found to be the best) Comes down—still down—and down With its centre on the crown
Of a mountain's eminence, While its wide circumference In easy drapery falls
Over hamlets, over halls, Wherever they may be—
O'er the strange woods—o'er the sea— Over spirits on the wing—
Over every drowsy thing— And buries them up quite In a labyrinth of light—
And then, how deep!—O, deep! Is the passion of their sleep.
In the morning they arise, And their moony covering Is soaring in the skies,
With the tempests as they toss, Like—almost any thing—
Or a yellow Albatross.
They use that moon no more For the same end as before—
Videlicet a tent—

Which I think extravagant: Its atomies, however, Into a shower dissever,
Of which those butterflies,
Of Earth, who seek the skies, And so come down again
(Never-contented things!) Have brought a specimen Upon their quivering wings.

1831.

 The Lake — To ——

IN spring of youth it was my lot To haunt of the wide earth a spot
The which I could not love the less— So lovely was the loneliness
Of a wild lake, with black rock bound, And the tall pines that tower'd around.

But when the Night had thrown her pall Upon that spot, as upon all,
And the mystic wind went by Murmuring in melody— Then— ah then I would awake To the terror of the lone lake.

Yet that terror was not fright, But a tremulous delight—
A feeling not the jewelled mine Could teach or bribe me to define—
Nor Love—although the Love were thine.

Death was in that poisonous wave, And in its gulf a fitting grave
For him who thence could solace bring To his lone imagining—
Whose solitary soul could make An Eden of that dim lake.

1827.

Evening Star

'TWAS noontide of summer, And midtime of night,
And stars, in their orbits, Shone pale, through the light
Of the brighter, cold moon. 'Mid planets her slaves,
Herself in the Heavens, Her beam on the waves.

I gazed awhile On her cold smile;
Too cold-too cold for me— There passed, as a shroud, A fleecy cloud,
And I turned away to thee,

Proud Evening Star, In thy glory afar
And dearer thy beam shall be; For joy to my heart
Is the proud part
Thou bearest in Heaven at night., And more I admire
Thy distant fire,
Than that colder, lowly light.

1827.

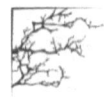 "The Happiest Day"

I
THE happiest day-the happiest hour
My seared and blighted heart hath known, The highest hope of pride and power,
I feel hath flown.
Of power! said I? Yes! such I ween But they have vanished long, alas!
The visions of my youth have been But let them pass.
III
And pride, what have I now with thee? Another brow may ev'n inherit
The venom thou hast poured on me Be still my spirit!
IV
The happiest day-the happiest hour Mine eyes shall see-have ever seen The brightest glance of pride and power I feet have been:
V
But were that hope of pride and power Now offered with the pain
Ev'n then I felt-that brightest hour I would not live again:
VI
For on its wing was dark alloy And as it fluttered-fell
 An essence-powerful to destroy A soul that knew it well.
1827.

Imitation

A dark unfathom'd tide Of interminable pride— A mystery, and a dream,
Should my early life seem;
I say that dream was fraught With a wild, and waking thought Of beings that have been, Which my spirit hath not seen, Had I let them pass me by, With a dreaming eye!
Let none of earth inherit That vision on my spirit;
Those thoughts I would control As a spell upon his soul:
For that bright hope at last And that light time have past,
And my worldly rest hath gone With a sigh as it pass'd on
I care not tho' it perish
With a thought I then did cherish. 1827.

Hymn To Aristogeiton And Harmodius

Translation from the Greek

I

WREATHED in myrtle, my sword I'll conceal Like those champions devoted and brave, When they plunged in the tyrant their steel, And to Athens deliverance gave.

II

Beloved heroes! your deathless souls roam In the joy breathing isles of the blest; Where the mighty of old have their home Where Achilles and Diomed rest

III

In fresh myrtle my blade I'll entwine, Like Harmodius, the gallant and good, When he made at the tutelar shrine
A libation of Tyranny's blood.

IV

Ye deliverers of Athens from shame! Ye avengers of Liberty's wrongs!
Endless ages shall cherish your fame, Embalmed in their echoing songs!
1827.

 Dreams

Oh! that my young life were a lasting dream! My spirit not awak'ning, till the beam
Of an Eternity should bring the morrow:
Yes! tho' that long dream were of hopeless sorrow, 'Twere better than the dull reality
Of waking life to him whose heart shall be, And hath been ever, on the chilly earth,
A chaos of deep passion from his birth!
But should it be—that dream eternally Continuing—as dreams have been to me
In my young boyhood—should it thus be given, 'Twere folly still to hope for higher Heaven!
For I have revell'd, when the sun was bright In the summer sky; in dreamy fields of light, And left unheedingly my very heart
In climes of mine imagining—apart
From mine own home, with beings that have been
Of mine own thought—what more could I have seen?

'Twas once & only once & the wild hour
From my rememberance shall not pass—some power Or spell had bound me—'twas the chilly wind
Came o'er me in the night & left behind Its image on my spirit, or the moon Shone on my slumbers in her lofty noon Too coldly—or the stars—howe'er it was
That dream was as that night wind—let it pass.

I have been happy—tho' but in a dream
I have been happy—& I love the theme— Dreams! in their vivid colouring of life— As in that fleeting, shadowy, misty strife Of semblance with reality which brings To the delirious eye more lovely things
Of Paradise & Love—& all our own!
Than young Hope in his sunniest hour hath known.

{From an earlier MS. Than in the book—ED.}

"In Youth I Have Known One"

How often we forget all time, when lone Admiring Nature's universal throne;
Her woods—her wilds—her mountains-the intense Reply of Hers to Our intelligence!

I

IN youth I have known one with whom the Earth In secret communing held-as he with it,
In daylight, and in beauty, from his birth: Whose fervid, flickering torch of life was lit
From the sun and stars, whence he had drawn forth A passionate light such for his spirit was fit
And yet that spirit knew-not in the hour
Of its own fervor-what had o'er it power.

II

Perhaps it may be that my mind is wrought
To a fever* by the moonbeam that hangs o'er, But I will half believe that wild light fraught
With more of sovereignty than ancient lore Hath ever told-or is it of a thought
The unembodied essence, and no more That with a quickening spell doth o'er us pass
As dew of the night-time, o'er the summer grass?

III

Doth o'er us pass, when, as th' expanding eye To the loved object-so the tear to the lid
Will start, which lately slept in apathy?

And yet it need not be—(that object) hid From us in life—but common—which doth lie
Each hour before us—but then only bid
With a strange sound, as of a harp-string broken T' awake us—'Tis a symbol and a token

IV

Of what in other worlds shall be—and given In beauty by our God, to those alone
Who otherwise would fall from life and Heaven Drawn by their heart's passion, and that tone,
That high tone of the spirit which hath striven
Though not with Faith—with godliness—whose throne With desperate energy 't hath beaten down;
Wearing its own deep feeling as a crown.

* Query "fervor"?—ED.

A PÆAN.

I.

How shall the burial rite be read?
The solemn song be sung?
The requiem for the loveliest dead, That ever died so young?

II.

Her friends are gazing on her, And on her gaudy bier,
And weep!—oh! to dishonor Dead beauty with a tear!

III.

They loved her for her wealth—
And they hated her for her pride— But she grew in feeble health,
And they love her—that she died.

IV.

They tell me (while they speak Of her "costly broider'd pall")

125

That my voice is growing weak— That I should not sing at all—

V.

Or that my tone should be Tun'd to such solemn song
So mournfully—so mournfully,
That the dead may feel no wrong.

VI.

But she is gone above,
With young Hope at her side, And I am drunk with love
Of the dead, who is my bride.—

VII.

Of the dead—dead who lies All perfum'd there,
With the death upon her eyes, And the life upon her hair.

VIII.

Thus on the coffin loud and long I strike—the murmur sent
Through the grey chambers to my song, Shall be the accompaniment.

IX.

Thou died'st in thy life's June— But thou did'st not die too fair:
Thou did'st not die too soon, Nor with too calm an air.

X.

From more than fiends on earth, Thy life and love are riven,
To join the untainted mirth
Of more than thrones in heaven—

XII.

Therefore, to thee this night I will no requiem raise,
But waft thee on thy flight, With a Pæan of old days.

Doubtful Poems

 # The Forest Reverie

'Tis said that when The hands of men
Tamed this primeval wood,
And hoary trees with groans of woe, Like warriors by an unknown foe, Were in their strength subdued,
The virgin Earth Gave instant birth To springs that ne'er did flow
That in the sun Did rivulets run,
And all around rare flowers did blow The wild rose pale
Perfumed the gale And the queenly lily adown the dale
(Whom the sun and the dew
And the winds did woo),
With the gourd and the grape luxuriant grew.

So when in tears The love of years
Is wasted like the snow, And the fine fibrils of its life
By the rude wrong of instant strife Are broken at a blow
Within the heart Do springs upstart
Of which it doth now know, And strange, sweet dreams, Like silent streams
That from new fountains overflow, With the earlier tide
Of rivers glide
Deep in the heart whose hope has died— Quenching the fires its ashes hide,—
Its ashes, whence will spring and grow Sweet flowers, ere long,
The rare and radiant flowers of song

Alone

From childhood's hour I have not been As others were—I have not seen
As others saw—I could not bring
My passions from a common spring— From the same source I have not taken My sorrow—I could not awaken
My heart to joy at the same tone— And all I lov'd—I lov'd alone— Then—in my childhood—in the dawn Of a most stormy life—was drawn From ev'ry depth of good and ill
The mystery which binds me still— From the torrent, or the fountain— From the red cliff of the mountain— From the sun that 'round me roll'd In its autumn tint of gold—
From the lightning in the sky As it pass'd me flying by—
From the thunder, and the storm— And the cloud that took the form (When the rest of Heaven was blue) Of a demon in my view—
{This poem is no longer considered doubtful as it was in 1903. Liberty has been taken to replace
the book version with an earlier, perhaps more original manuscript version—Ed}

 To Isadore

I
BENEATH the vine-clad eaves, Whose shadows fall before Thy lowly cottage door
Under the lilac's tremulous leaves— Within thy snowy claspeèd hand
The purple flowers it bore..
Last eve in dreams, I saw thee stand, Like queenly nymphs from Fairy-land— Enchantress of the flowery wand,
Most beauteous Isadore!

II
And when I bade the dream Upon thy spirit flee,
Thy violet eyes to me Upturned, did overflowing seem With the deep, untold delight
Of Love's serenity;
Thy classic brow, like lilies white And pale as the Imperial Night Upon her throne, with stars bedight,
Enthralled my soul to thee!

III
Ah I ever I behold
Thy dreamy, passionate eyes, Blue as the languid skies

Hung with the sunset's fringe of gold; Now strangely clear thine image grows,
And olden memories
Are startled from their long repose Like shadows on the silent snows

When suddenly the night-wind blows Where quiet moonlight ties.

IV
Like music heard in dreams,
Like strains of harps unknown, Of birds forever flown

Audible as the voice of streams That murmur in some leafy dell,
I hear thy gentlest tone,
And Silence cometh with her spell
Like that which on my tongue doth dwell, When tremulous in dreams I tell
My love to thee alone!

V
In every valley heard, Floating from tree to tree, Less beautiful to, me,
The music of the radiant bird, Than artless accents such as thine
Whose echoes never flee!
Ah! how for thy sweet voice I pine:— For uttered in thy tones benign (Enchantress!) this rude name of mine

Doth seem a melody!

 The Village Street

IN these rapid, restless shadows, Once I walked at eventide,
When a gentle, silent maiden, Walked in beauty at my side
She alone there walked beside me All in beauty, like a bride.

Pallidly the moon was shining On the dewy meadows nigh;
On the silvery, silent rivers,
On the mountains far and high On the ocean's star-lit waters,
Where the winds a-weary die.

Slowly, silently we wandered From the open cottage door,
Underneath the elm's long branches To the pavement bending o'er; Underneath the mossy willow
And the dying sycamore.

With the myriad stars in beauty
All bedight, the heavens were seen, Radiant hopes were bright around me, Like the light of stars serene;
Like the mellow midnight splendor Of the Night's irradiate queen.

Audibly the elm-leaves whispered Peaceful, pleasant melodies,
Like the distant murmured music
Of unquiet, lovely seas:
While the winds were hushed in slumber In the fragrant flowers and trees.

Wondrous and unwonted beauty Still adorning all did seem,

While I told my love in fables
'Neath the willows by the stream; Would the heart have kept unspoken
Love that was its rarest dream!

Instantly away we wandered In the shadowy twilight tide,
She, the silent, scornful maiden, Walking calmly at my side,

With a step serene and stately, All in beauty, all in pride.

Vacantly I walked beside her.
On the earth mine eyes were cast; Swift and keen there came unto me
Ritter memories of the past On me, like the rain in Autumn
On the dead leaves, cold and fast.

Underneath the elms we parted, By the lowly cottage door;
One brief word alone was uttered Never on our lips before;
And away I walked forlornly, Broken-hearted evermore.

Slowly, silently I loitered, Homeward, in the night, alone;
Sudden anguish bound my spirit, That my youth had never known;
Wild unrest, like that which cometh
When the Night's first dream hath flown.

Now, to me the elm-leaves whisper Mad, discordant melodies,
And keen melodies like shadows Haunt the moaning willow trees,
And the sycamores with laughter Mock me in the nightly breeze.

Sad and pale the Autumn moonlight Through the sighing foliage streams;
And each morning, midnight shadow,

Shadow of my sorrow seems; Strive, O heart, forget thine idol!
And, O soul, forget thy dreams!

www.ingramcontent.com/pod-product-compliance
Lightning Source LLC
Chambersburg PA
CBHW030040100526
44590CB00011B/280